STICK TECHNIQUE

The Essential Guide for the Modern Drummer

by Bill Bachman

Modern Drummer Publisher / CEO - **David Frangioni**

President - **David Hakim**

Director of Content / Editor - **Mark Griffith**

Senior Art Director - **Scott Beinstock**

Editorial - **Michael Finkelstein**

Archivist - **Felipe Laverde**

Edited by Michael Dawson

Design and layout by Gerald Vitale

Cover photos by Rick Malkin

Interior photos by Rick Malkin, Leslie Voorheis, and Sally Somers

Published by:
Modern Drummer Media, LLC.
1279 W Palmetto Park Rd
PO Box 276064
Boca Raton, FL 33427

Subscribe to *Modern Drummer*: moderndrummer.com/subscribe

For videos, visit and subscribe to the "Modern Drummer Official" YouTube channel

Table of Contents

FOREWORD

Welcome to *Stick Technique: The Essential Guide for the Modern Drummer*. The goal of this book is to help you develop hands that are loose, stress free, and ready to play anything that comes to your mind. The book is for everyone who plays with sticks, regardless of whether you're focusing primarily on drumset, orchestral percussion, or the rudimental style of drumming. The book is designed to get you playing essential techniques correctly and as quickly as possible.

Stick Technique is broken up into three main sections: Technique, Top Twelve Rudiments, and Chops Builders. In the Technique section, we'll take an in-depth look at the most practical and essential grips and playing techniques. We'll discuss the advantages and disadvantages of each, as well as why to learn them and when to use them.

The Top Twelve Rudiments section includes the ten rudiments covered in my Strictly Technique series in *Modern Drummer* magazine, plus two additional rudiments. All of the essential hand motions you'll need to know are included within these twelve rudiments.

Also from my *Modern Drummer* magazine articles, the Chops Builders section includes exercises that are designed to build great technique while also sneaking in a bit of very useful vocabulary.

Finally, there is a bonus section to build coordination and independence between the hands for drumset applications.

The exercises in the book are easy to figure out so that you can focus on the technique and not the exercise itself. (They may be easy to play, but they're hard to play *perfectly*.) Be sure to extrapolate and perfect any small parts of the exercises that give you trouble. There's no sense working on the whole exercise if each section isn't where it needs to be. You should also memorize the exercises. If they're not engrained in your memory then you haven't practiced them enough to get the real value from each.

Once you've gotten through *Stick Technique* you'll find yourself playing with better sound quality, while expending less energy and remaining injury free. Your technique will be more relaxed, allowing you to play more musically, dynamically, and faster than ever before—and, best of all, you'll never have to think about technique on the gig! Your hands will be ready to play anything, automatically using the technique that offers the path of least resistance so you can concentrate on making music. Practice smart, practice a lot, and have fun doing it!

Bill Bachman

ACKNOWLEDGEMENTS

Thanks to my wife, Vita, and daughter, Sophia, for their love and inspiration, to my parents for putting up with the noise in the early years, to the many teachers and fellow drummers who have shared their talents with me along the way, to my many students for being guinea pigs for these methods for so many years, to Mike Dawson at *Modern Drummer* for his editing skills and patience in taking the time to max this book out, and to the Lord for giving me (among other things) such endless joy using only two sticks and a pad.

Section 1: TECHNIQUE

INTRODUCTION

First of all, let's start with a disclaimer: Technique is just a means to an end, and that end is making music without having to think about technique. If you're thinking about technique on the gig, you'll sound that way to the audience. If you're playing from the heart, you'll sound like you're expressing yourself openly—as long as your technique is at a level where the execution (or lack of execution) of your ideas doesn't ruin the experience for the listener. Technique leads to ability, and ability leads to vocabulary. Having more than enough technique, ability, and vocabulary is a good thing, since the more you have, the more you'll be able to draw from when the time is right.

Using proper technique will also prevent injury. Most of the time, drumming-related injuries occur when you work too hard and ask too much of the body. Many drummers hold on to the sticks too tightly and use too much force by playing "through" the drums and cymbals, which often leads to injury and broken equipment. Proper technique will allow you to play loosely and with more velocity, which results in more sound, improved flow, better feel, more endurance, more speed, and *no* injuries.

A lot of drummers ask, "Which technique is best?" The correct answer is any of them—depending on the situation. All too often a certain technique gets accepted as being "better" than another. While this seems to simplify things, it actually limits your options. In this book we're going to look at *all* of the essential techniques that a well-rounded drummer needs to master in order to play well and in the most efficient manner possible.

Along with discussing various grips and fulcrums, in the following chapters we'll dive into the following stroke techniques:

Free stroke (aka full stroke or legato stroke). This loose, rebounding stroke is the foundation of efficient drumming technique. It's used when playing successive strokes at the same stick height and dynamic level.

Alley-oop. This is a wrist/finger combination technique that's used when playing diddles (double strokes) and triple strokes. This technique is necessary at tempos where the wrists can't play multiple-note combinations without tensing up.

Downstroke, tap, and upstroke. Downstrokes and upstrokes are just like free strokes, except that after you hit the drum, the stick heights are modified in order to play subsequent strokes at a different dynamic level. Taps are low free strokes.

Moeller whip stroke. This technique involves playing downstrokes and upstrokes from the forearm when the wrist would otherwise get overworked and stiffen up. The Moeller whip stroke is crucial for playing accent patterns with a smooth and effortless flow, especially at fast tempos.

So, how do you choose when to use a certain technique? The technique you use will be determined by the type of rudiment or pattern being played, the instrument being played, and the tempo. Once the various techniques are mastered, your hands will automatically choose the one that allows you to perform in the most effective and efficient way possible.

The bottom line is that in order to develop a wide vocabulary on the drums, you need to have a lot of techniques at your disposal. Building technique requires thousands of correct repetitions ("perfect practice") in order to train your muscle memory. While there are no shortcuts to developing good technique, the material in this book is designed to help you get there as quickly as possible.

MATCHED GRIP

Matched grip simply means that the hands hold the sticks in a mirror image of one another. There are important variations within matched grip, however, both in terms of the hand angles and fulcrums (pivot points) that are used. The main grip variations are German, French, and American.

German grip involves holding the hands flat and favors wrist use over finger use. French grip involves holding the hands more vertically, with the thumb on top, and favors finger use over wrist use. American grip falls in the middle of German and French in order to utilize the advantages of both.

The common fulcrums for matched grip are between the thumb and the first finger or between the thumb and second finger. The first-finger fulcrum is generally better for speed and finesse at lower stick heights (finger micromanagement), while the second-finger fulcrum is generally better for bigger strokes and for more power (wrist/forearm-driven). Quite often the fulcrum will be located somewhere in-between the two and will adjust automatically according to the demand put on the hands. Each hand position and fulcrum point within the matched grip variations has advantages and disadvantages, so it's good to master each of them in order to be prepared to use the most appropriate technique for a particular situation.

German Grip

German grip is the position where the hands are held flat. Grasp a drumstick between your thumb and first finger. Lightly wrap your other fingers around the stick and set your hand down on a table. That's it! You'll notice that if you keep the wrist relaxed in a natural position, the angle of the stick will be somewhat turned in and the butt end of the stick will jut out a bit to the side of the hand. The sticks will generally form a V at about a 90-degree angle.

German grip

German grip is great for wrist use, downstrokes, and the Moeller whip stroke. It favors wrist use over finger use, since the fingers have a narrower range of motion in this position.

Because the palm of the hand is held directly over the stick in German grip, the fingers can squeeze the stick against the palm to stop the rebound when playing downstrokes. (I'll later refer to this as the "brakes.") German grip is also great for the Moeller whip stroke because the butt end of the stick can protrude past the wrist when the forearm is raised in preparation for the stroke.

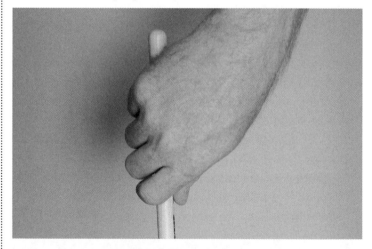

One thing to watch out for with German grip is an extrawide V setup where the sticks are turned in to form an angle greater than 90 degrees.

What *not* to do

This extra-wide position forces you to play with an exaggerated inward wrist rotation and less of the desired up-and-down motion. The up-and-down wrist motion has more power and leverage. Another disadvantage of improper German grip is that the wider the V, the less range of motion you'll have for your fingers.

French Grip

French grip is the position where the hands are held vertically, with the thumb on top and in line with the sticks.

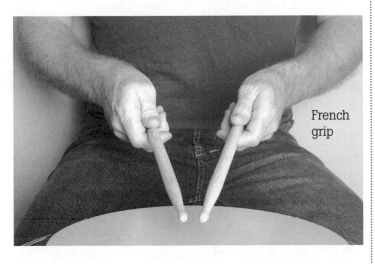

French grip

To get into French grip, hold out your hand as though you're going to shake hands with someone, and then add the stick between your thumb and first finger, making sure that the end of the first finger curls upward somewhat so the stick can't roll out. Lightly curl the rest of the fingers underneath. That's it!

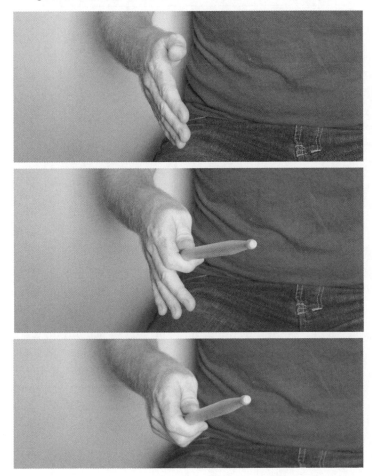

With the wrist relaxed in its natural position, the angle of the stick will be somewhat turned out relative to the forearm, and the butt end of the stick will be located at the inside of the wrist. The sticks will generally form a very narrow V at about a 20-degree angle or close to parallel.

French grip favors finger use over wrist use, since the fingers have a wider range of motion.

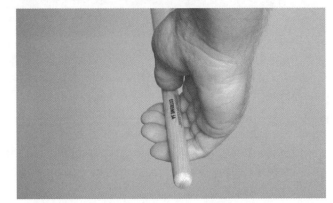

In French grip, the wrist has a narrower range of motion and relies partially on an outward rotation. French grip is good for free strokes because the "brakes" (palms of the hands) are now unavailable to stop the stick on the rebound. The stick breathes and resonates well when held in this position, which is why French grip is so commonly used when playing timpani or the ride cymbal. It's a great grip to use when you want a loose, wide-open sound from a freely rebounding stick or mallet.

One thing to watch out for when using French grip is an open, claw-looking hand, where the stick turns out excessively relative to the thumb. In this improper position, there's very little control available since the stick isn't stabilized within the fulcrum.

What *not* to do

American Grip

American grip is where the hand angle is in between German (flat) and French (vertical). The hands and thumbs are at about a 45-degree angle. With American grip, the first knuckle of the first finger is the highest point of the hand, and the stick is in line with the forearm or turned slightly inward. The sticks will generally form a V at about a 50-degree angle.

American grip

American grip is great for almost everything, since the wrists can turn up and down with a wide range of motion, the "brakes" are readily available for down-strokes, the butt end of the sticks won't hit the underside of the wrists when playing Moeller whip strokes, and the fingers have a relatively wide range of motion. Since the thumb is positioned towards the topside of the stick, it can open up a bit to be more on the side (like in German grip) when the stick comes up, and you can squeeze it in a bit to be more on top (like French grip) when the sticks are lower and when more finger control is required.

Choosing a Grip

If you had to choose only one grip to use exclusively, the American grip would be the winner. However, if you limit yourself to American grip, you will miss out on the advantages of the other two, especially French grip for ride-cymbal playing. The ability to play each of the grips will allow you to use different parts of your body for different drumming tasks.

On a related note, many drummers find that they inadvertently slice (hit the drum at an angle instead of perpendicularly) when they play. This is often related to whichever matched-grip wrist motion you favor. For instance, if you slice inward, you can flatten out your hand more toward German grip, and the stick will start to travel vertically. If you slice outward, turn your hands more vertically, toward French grip. Ideally, you want to be able to hold your hands everywhere in between French and German grip while maintaining perpendicular strokes.

Stick Angles Relative to the Drum

Both sticks should point down toward the drum at about a 10-degree angle.

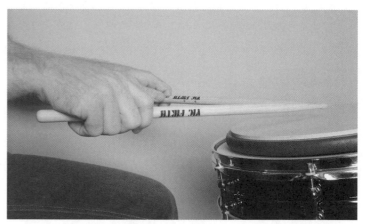

Matching this stick angle in both hands is important so that both sticks get the same sound and rebound out of the drum. The flatter the angle the sticks are relative to the drum, the more rebound. The steeper the angle, the less rebound. While it might seem that the more rebound the better, it's good to have some leverage over the stick for when you want to play down into the drum or to set yourself up for downstrokes that stop lower to the drum. The 10-degree angle gives you this leverage while still maintaining great rebound.

Fulcrums

The most important part of any grip is the fulcrum (pivot point). We use three fulcrums when drumming: the elbow, the wrist, and the axis between the thumb and first or second finger. When we discuss fulcrums in this book, we'll always be referring to the rotational axis between the thumb and first or second finger.

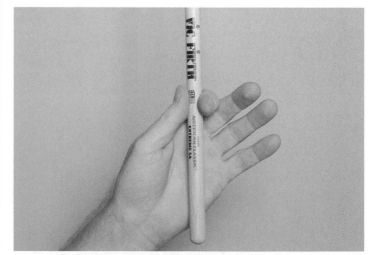

It's important that the thumb and first or second finger be located directly across from each other so that the stick can pivot freely. This allows the remaining fingers to be used to help move the stick instead of gripping it. Without a good fulcrum, you'll never develop the finesse that comes from incorporating the fingers, and you'll be limiting your potential.

In American grip, the thumb should be a bit on top of

the stick so that it's in a position where it can push the stick down when extra leverage is needed.

As you look down at the stick in your hand, the V formed where your first finger and thumb meet should be centered over the middle of the stick.

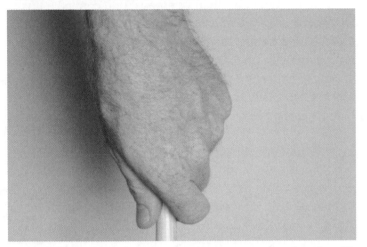

When you raise the stick all the way up, the thumb will naturally move to the side. If your thumb always stays positioned on the side of the stick, or if the thumb hangs lower, you'll have difficulty playing downstrokes and roll patterns where you need to press down in the front of the grip.

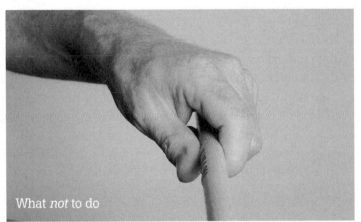

What *not* to do

Players who use this problematic fulcrum will have to compensate for the lack of control by holding the stick more with their fingers, which limits the ability to use the fingers to help play the stick.

As a general rule, your fulcrum should be located a little less than a third of the way from the back of the stick. This is the sweet spot where the stick rebounds as much as possible on its own. You'll want to hold the stick at this point so that it can do as much of the work as possible.

Each hand should have the fulcrum located at the same spot on the stick; otherwise the sound and volume between the hands will be different. If you find that one hand is choking up higher than the other, quite often the choked-up stick is in the hand with less-developed finger technique. A choked-up stick will have a darker/quieter/ stiffer sound because it's being played with more wrist motion.

There's a lot of discussion about whether or not to have a gap in your grip between the thumb and the hand. This

relates to the choice of using a first- or second-finger fulcrum (which will be explained in the next section). As a general rule, a first-finger fulcrum will leave no gap, while a second-finger fulcrum will.

Most players who grip the sticks too tightly will have no gap between the thumb and hand, regardless of their fulcrum choice. While the lack of gap is a common symptom of playing tightly, I've seen players try to create a gap in order to play "looser," but they're still using a first-finger fulcrum. This results in a lot of extra tension in the hand, because they have to squeeze the stick extra-hard in the fulcrum so that it doesn't slide up into the gap, plus the back fingers are now needed to stabilize the stick where they would otherwise be used to play it.

No matter which fulcrum you use, the stick should be held just tightly enough to remain in your hand. If the stick slides, or falls out of the fulcrum, you simply need to apply a bit more pressure with the thumb in order to keep the stick secure in the sweet spot. With relaxed hands, the sticks will feel heavy as they do a lot of the work for you.

First-Finger or Second-Finger Fulcrum?

There's some debate about the fulcrum's ideal location. Some players prefer to hold the stick between the thumb and first finger, while others prefer to hold the stick between the thumb and second finger. Quite often you'll want to play using a combination of the two, which some call the "three-point fulcrum," but favoring either a first- or second-finger fulcrum will be necessary at times, depending on the vocabulary you're trying to play.

Both the first- and second-finger fulcrums have advantages and disadvantages, and a well-trained drummer should have both options at his or her disposal. Once both fulcrum options are learned, the fulcrum you use will change automatically based on the physical demands of the music.

It's important that the first-finger fulcrum be well developed, because it's ideal for finesse and high-speed and lower-dynamic playing at lower stick heights. The end of the first finger, which is underneath the fulcrum, can move the stick very quickly and very lightly with very little linear movement. This is why when playing at high speeds with a light touch it's common for the front two fingers to control the stick while the back two fingers do very little work. In this situation, the thumb will rise to the topside of the stick a bit, and the gap between the thumb and hand will be eliminated in order to hold the stick in the first knuckle joint of the index finger so that the tip of the index finger has maximum access to play the stick.

First-finger fulcrum

A second-finger fulcrum transfers more of the wrist's energy to the stick for a more powerful stroke. This fulcrum is also preferable when playing with the Moeller whip stroke, where you want as much of the whip motion as possible to flow from the arm and hand into the stick.

Second-finger fulcrum

I always start by teaching the first-finger fulcrum because it's easy to fall back to the second-finger fulcrum when finger finesse isn't required. If, however, you start by learning the second-finger fulcrum, you'll have a more difficult time getting the first finger to function when needed.

A good exercise for getting your fulcrum together is

what I call the "first-finger fulcrum isolator."

Hold the stick near the front end and play the back of the stick on the bottom of your forearm, using just the first-finger fulcrum. The top of your hand should remain still. (Don't cheat by using the wrist!) If your first-finger fulcrum is out of position or not working correctly, this exercise is nearly impossible to execute, so it forces you to develop good technique. The exercise will make your forearm burn pretty quickly. Later you'll add the other fingers to help move the stick, which makes the first finger's job much easier.

Grip/Fulcrum Conclusion

It's good to have every grip and fulcrum option at your disposal, since each has its advantages. I tend to use the first- and second-finger fulcrums about equally, and I employ every hand position between the extremes of French and German grips.

I also break my own grip and fulcrum rules from time to time. For instance, when I play rimshots on the snare, I tend to hold the stick lightly between my second and third fingers. And when I crash a cymbal with no need to play anything immediately afterward, I sometimes hold the stick loosely, like a bicycle handlebar. If I'm not going to use my fingers to play the stick, then I have no need for a proper fulcrum. Of course, it's important to learn the rules before you can break them. So get on it!

TRADITIONAL GRIP

Traditional grip is where the left stick is held underhanded, while the right stick is held the same as in matched grip. Traditional grip goes back hundreds of years, when drums were held on a sling over the shoulder. This position caused the drum to hang in front of the body at an angle. Rather than lift the entire left arm to get the left hand into playing position on these tilted drums, players used an underhanded technique so that the left arm could hang comfortably. It's rare to see anyone playing a drum on a sling anymore, but the grip still exists.

Some drummers who play traditional grip set up their drums so that they're tilting away from their bodies or angled to the right in order to accommodate the left hand's position. Traditional grip is more difficult to develop than

matched, and I feel that it's easier to learn *after* a solid foundation is built with matched grip.

There are many mechanical disadvantages to playing on a flat drum with traditional grip. Here are some common arguments against traditional grip:

1. It's difficult to play with a balanced sound when holding one stick overhand and the other underhand.

2. There are different amounts of flesh on each stick, which affects stick resonance.

3. The left stick has a much more limited range of motion and almost no capacity for lateral motion.

4. There are fewer muscles used in the left hand to spread the workload.

5. There are fewer fingers available to play the stick.

The list goes on, but it's possible to overcome these disadvantages and play extremely well with traditional grip. Plus traditional grip has its own feel. So if it works for you, run with it!

Traditional Grip Technique

To get going with traditional grip, start by holding out your left hand as if you're going to shake somebody's left hand.

Place the stick in the webbing between the thumb and first finger at about a 135-degree angle relative to the forearm. The stick should contact the hand a little bit behind the sweet spot. Be sure not to let the stick turn inward to form a 90-degree angle relative to the forearm.

Next, curl in the ring finger and pinkie and let the stick rest on the cuticle of the ring finger between the nail and the flesh. It's ideal for the stick to contact the finger here and not farther back, since there's more leverage to lift the stick when it's held near the end of the finger.

Now curl your first two fingers over the stick and hold your thumb against the first finger so that it forms a "T." It's important to maintain this connection between the thumb and first finger. You also want to avoid closing the fingers so that the angle of the stick is brought inward. You can always check this by looking for a 135-degree angle between the thumb and stick.

With matched grip, it's common to focus on symmetrical stick angles relative to the body. With traditional grip, however, I don't recommend angling in the right stick in order to mirror the angle of the left stick unless symmetry is required, like when playing on a marching snare. Remember that the more angled in the right stick is, the less access the fingers have to play the stick.

Both sticks should point down toward the drum at about a 10-degree angle. Matching this stick angle with traditional grip can be challenging, since the right hand is overhand and the left underhand. But if the two sticks approach the drum at different angles, you get two different sounds, and the rebound will differ as well. The tendency for inexperienced traditional-grip players is for the left stick to approach the drum at a steeper angle, which greatly decreases rebound.

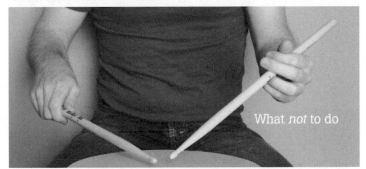

What *not* to do

In traditional grip, the left wrist rotates while the right wrist moves up and down. The left hand's first two fingers and thumb are used to play the stick for finger control (though quite often the middle finger does nothing and is just along for the ride), and they hold the stick close to the drum when playing downstrokes. The ring finger on the left hand is used as a resting point to stop the stick, which is similar to the palm on the right hand (the "brakes"). The left-hand ring finger is also used to push the stick back up to the starting position. The left-hand pinkie is used simply to support the ring finger, where with matched grip the pinkie helps move the stick.

Traditional Grip Fulcrum

The fulcrum (or pivot point) of the left hand in traditional grip is simple, and there's only one choice. The key is figuring out how far up or down on the stick to hold it so that it bounces as much as possible on its own. Experiment with holding the stick farther up on the neck, and notice when the stroke gets smaller and loses power and rebound potential. Then try holding the stick farther back, and notice when it feels awkward in the hand and again loses rebound potential. There's a middle ground where the stick rebounds the most, and this is your sweet spot. Place the sweet spot just in front of where the stick touches the webbing between your thumb and first finger.

If you find that the stick spins or starts to gradually slide out of your hand, focus on keeping the thumb held against the index finger to form a T. You may also need to add a bit more pressure at that connection. Just make sure you don't tighten up in other areas of the hand. The stick still needs to be loose and have freedom to move within the hand.

FREE STROKE

The free stroke, which is also commonly referred to as the full stroke or the legato stroke, is the most important technique you should learn, as it's the foundation for almost every other stroke type. The free stroke is basically a dribble of the stick where you throw the stick down toward the drum and then let it rebound off the drumhead so that it returns to the height where it started. Free strokes should be used for everything played at one stick height where there's no logical reason to hold the stick down near the drumhead. Free strokes require a solid fulcrum and very relaxed hands. Some drummers even feel as if they're cheating when they first learn to execute this stroke.

A properly played free stroke proves two things about your technique. First, it shows that the stroke was played with enough velocity into the drum so that it could rebound back up to the starting point. Second, it shows that the hand is relaxed enough that the stick could rebound without being disrupted by tension. Practicing free strokes is a great way to loosen up your hands and improve your consistency and sound quality.

The more you hold on to the stick and manipulate its motion, the greater the chance for human error and inconsistency, and the more stress you put on your hands. Conversely, if you relax and let physics carry the workload, your playing will have increased flow and consistency, and you'll put less stress on the hands.

Volume is determined more by how *fast* you move the stick to hit the drum than it is by how hard you strike. To get the most sound out of your instrument, focus on playing big and loose free strokes with high velocity, instead of simply hitting hard with a lot of inertia through the drumhead. You'll not only produce more volume with less effort, but you'll also be able to play faster and with more endurance. Plus you'll do less damage to your hands and to your equipment.

Free-Stroke Technique for Matched Grip

To play a free stroke, start with the sticks held in the "up" position, with the wrists turned up and the fingers held partially open.

The "up" position

Throw the stick down toward the drum, using the wrist and all four fingers to accelerate it. With the hand held loose, let the stick hit the drum with all of its velocity and freely rebound back up to where it started. The key is to quickly accelerate the stick and then immediately relax the hand. It's helpful to think about playing big strokes where you throw the stick down fast—but not hard.

When playing free strokes, the butt end of the stick should never hit the palm of your hand, or else some of the stick's energy will be absorbed into the hand and won't make it to the drum. If the fingers hold the stick against the palm, there will be extra tension in the hand, which results in less acceleration and a stiffer sound. When everything is working properly, the stick should feel heavy and should resonate fully with a high-pitched sound.

It's very important to locate the fulcrum on the stick at the point where it rebounds most freely. If you choke up too far, the stick doesn't rebound very well. Likewise, if you hold the stick too far back, the stick doesn't rebound well and you also get an uncomfortable vibration from the stick into the back fingers. The fulcrum should be located where the stick does the most work for you, and the stick should be held just tightly enough that you don't drop it. In matched grip, be sure to allow the end of the first finger to operate separately from the fulcrum point so that you can use the tip of the finger to play the stick.

Free strokes can be played with various ratios of wrist to finger. Favoring the wrist over the fingers will result in bigger and louder strokes, since the stick moves in a larger arch.

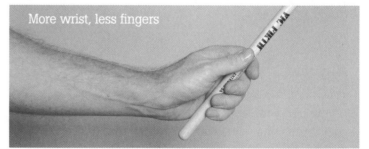

More wrist, less fingers

Favoring finger use, which focuses on the fulcrum between the thumb and first or second finger, results in smaller strokes that can be desirable for greater finesse and speed, especially at lower stick heights and softer volumes.

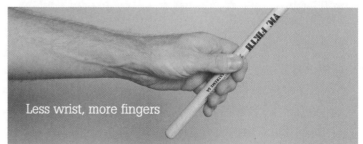

Less wrist, more fingers

It's ideal to have the technical ability to play at either end of the spectrum (finger or wrist strokes) and to have the ability to gradually morph from one to the other.

Free-Stroke Technique for Traditional Grip

Once the free stroke is mastered with matched grip, it's time to look at how to play this technique with traditional grip (if desired). Keep in mind that the same physics apply. To play the free stroke with the left hand, start with the stick in the up position and then rotate the wrist, accelerating the stick down toward the drum using the thumb and first two fingers. With the hand held loosely, the stick will strike the drum with all of its velocity and then rebound back to the height where it started. The free stroke's rebound can actually push the stick farther back than the wrist can naturally rotate. This will help to gradually increase the range of motion within your traditional grip.

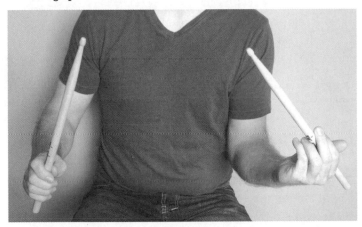

When playing free strokes, it's important not to hold the stick against the ring finger in the left hand. The ring finger and pinkie function the same way as the palm does in matched grip (the "brakes"). If the stick continually touches the ring finger, then the stick is being accelerated only by the rotation of the wrist and not by the thumb and first two fingers on top of the stick. Along with the thumb, sometimes both fingers on top help accelerate the stick. Other times, the first finger does most of the work, while the middle finger hangs off the stick somewhat. This is okay. Just make sure that the middle finger is near its proper position, since you'll need it for other techniques.

Developing the Free Stroke in Matched Grip

When first learning the free stroke, most drummers feel they're cheating, or they feel somewhat out of control since they're used to doing so much more work. "More work" simply means more tension, and more tension generally slows down your strokes and robs you of sound quality and flow. What initially feels out of control and lazy will become comfortable once you've practiced it long enough to achieve the proper muscle memory.

Begin by practicing individual free strokes that start and stop past vertical. To get past vertical, you must open your

fingers a bit. You want your fingers to be in a position to play the stick instead of holding it. Don't rob yourself of the potential speed and flow generated by using the fingers in addition to the wrist to accelerate the stroke. (When playing free strokes with French grip, limit the stick height to as high as the thumb will allow without the fulcrum changing.) Focus more on stick's return to the "up" position than the hand action used to play the free stroke, since the stick's motion *after* striking the drum tends to be a telltale sign of whether or not the free stroke was played correctly.

Once your individual free strokes are comfortable and consistent, start stringing them together as consecutive dribbles of the stick. After these consecutive free strokes are feeling comfortable and are consistently returning past vertical, practice them at lower stick heights. As the tempo goes up, the stick heights consequently come down.

Be careful not to neglect the wrist once you're comfortable opening the fingers and using them to accelerate the stroke. If you find that your pinkie can't reach the stick, or it barely touches the side of the stick, then you need to raise the wrist higher so that the pinkie can reach the front of the stick. This will result in a healthy balance of wrist and finger use for playing free strokes.

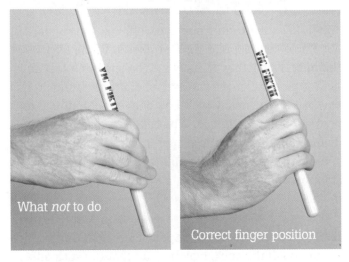

What *not* to do

Correct finger position

I always have students begin by playing free strokes using just the fulcrum and the end of the first finger, while the three back fingers hang completely off the stick. From there we add the fingers one at a time.

This hand position isolates the foundation of the free stroke, which is the fulcrum and the end of the first finger. Once the first finger is playing the stick well, I have students add one finger at a time, making sure that the sound and flow don't change throughout.

Developing the Free Stroke in Traditional Grip

To develop the free stroke in traditional grip, start by rotating the wrist, with the stick held only in the fulcrum. (The thumb and fingers should point away from your body.) Even though this isn't proper traditional grip, it's worth practicing by holding the stick in this manner in order to identify the feeling of a good rebound from the ideal fulcrum point.

Next, add the thumb on top of the stick so that the stick is held at the proper angle relative to the forearm (about 135 degrees). The stick will now be held against the fleshy webbing between the thumb and fingers and the pad of the thumb. Practice dribbling free strokes in this position, using the pad of the thumb on top of the stick to drive the stick. The fingers should continue to point outward.

Work this thumb-only position until you can comfortably play single, double, and triple strokes with the stick rebounding smoothly on its own. You shouldn't feel any pain in the hand, since the impact of the stick should be absorbed by the fleshy webbing between the thumb and fingers and not the bones. What often sets apart an advanced traditional-grip player from someone who can simply turn the wrist is the ability to finesse the stick using the thumb in conjunction with the fingers on top of the stick.

Once your free strokes are working well using just the thumb, it's time to add the fingers. Start with the two fingers on top of the stick, making sure that the stick still rebounds freely and loosely. Check that the thumb and first finger are held together in a T. Doing so will help secure the fulcrum and prevent the stick from sliding up or down in your hand. You should be able to play continuous free strokes while randomly adding and taking away the top two fingers without the stick's flow being affected.

Finally, curl your two bottom fingers under the stick. The bottom two fingers actually do nothing while playing free strokes, though it's okay for the stick to lightly tap the ring finger's nail. It's very important that the stick not be squeezed between the second and third fingers. This would result in a tight grip where the top two fingers and thumb can't help accelerate the stick.

Another method that's helpful for developing traditional-grip free strokes is the overhand dribble. With the palm facing the floor, let the stick sit in the fleshy spot between the thumb and first finger, and then dribble the stick using the first two fingers on top of the stick. While a bit tricky at first, this exercise is quite helpful in developing finger control in traditional grip.

Troubleshooting

There are four common mistakes that many drummers make when playing free strokes.

1. Picking up the stick. Many drummers are so used to holding onto the stick tightly that they're working twice as hard as necessary. Imagine dribbling a basketball. Even though it may feel out of control at first, let the stick be free to rebound on its own.

2. The butt end of the stick hits the palm. The palms (and the ring finger and pinkie in traditional grip) are the brakes and can only slow down the stroke. If the stick is held against the brakes, the flow and sound choke off, and you can accelerate the stick only with the wrist. The fingers should be used to help play the stick instead of gripping it.

3. Playing with mostly fingers and very little wrist. Remember that the more you incorporate the wrist, the bigger the sound. The greater the wrist-to-finger ratio, the bigger the arch in the stroke, which results in greater velocity and more power.

4. Not using all four fingers to play the stick. When playing free strokes, the wrist should come up enough that all four fingers can reach the front of the stick. If your pinkie is on the side of the stick, then it can't participate in the stroke. Raise your wrist so the pinkie can get in on the action.

ALLEY-OOP

The alley-oop technique is what I call a wrist/finger free-stroke combination used for playing double strokes (diddles) and triple strokes. While it can be likened to the push/pull technique, which is a wrist stroke followed by a finger stroke, the alley-oop isn't intended for playing ongoing, evenly metered strokes. It's a technique for playing short bursts of two or three notes.

The initial stroke (alley) is played mainly from the wrist and uses a higher stick height with slower acceleration. The second stroke (oop) is played from the fingers and uses a lower stick height and faster acceleration in order to match the volume of the initial stroke. The alley-oop requires quick finger technique in order to accelerate the second stroke. When playing low doubles, it might be helpful to think of the alley-oop as a drop-catch technique where the hand drops the stick and then the fingers catch it into the palm, adding a bit of velocity to the second stroke. The fingers also have to relax after their strokes so that the stick can bounce up to the starting position. As complicated as this may sound, the alley-oop technique is the best way to play double strokes and triple strokes, and it will start happening automatically as you increase the tempo of your free-stroke doubles and triples.

Many drummers struggle with double and triple strokes. The problems often fall into one of two categories: relying too heavily on bounce or stroking each beat entirely from the wrist. If you simply bounce the second and third strokes, they will sound weaker than the first stroke because they have less velocity going into the drum. If you stroke everything from the wrist, your speed will be limited. Plus you'll lose sound quality, your hands will get tight, and you'll risk wrist injury since you'll be asking the wrists to do too much.

Once you've developed strong finger control, you'll not only be able to play well-balanced doubles and triples, but you'll also be able to crescendo within them to add dynamic contour within roll patterns. It takes time and practice to develop the ability to play the finger strokes with good velocity, but it's worth it.

Alley-Oop Technique in Matched Grip

To play alley-oop doubles, play a free stroke at a high stick height, using mainly the wrist, and let the stick rebound back up as much as possible before playing the second stroke.

When playing very slow doubles, both notes are played as identical free strokes, since there's time for the hand and stick to come all the way back up. As you play faster doubles, however, there's not enough time for the hand to come all the way up to play the second stroke. This is where the alley-oop technique becomes necessary.

At faster tempos, the second stroke (which is also a free stroke) will need to be played with more fingers than wrist,

from a lower stick height. You'll need to move the stick with greater velocity in order to match the volume of the first stroke, since the first stroke was played at a higher stick height. Remember that volume is determined by the *speed* of stroke, not the stick height.

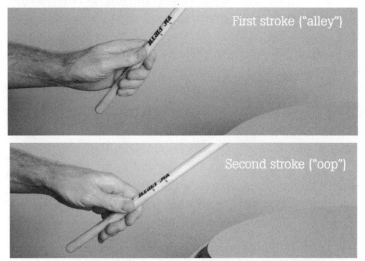

First stroke ("alley")

Second stroke ("oop")

To summarize the alley-oop technique, the first note should be played mainly with the wrist and the second stroke should be played mainly with the fingers (though the wrist can move a bit for the second stroke too). As you increase the speed of the double or triple stroke, the stick height will naturally drop with each subsequent stroke. But if you play the rebound strokes with higher velocity than the first (using the fingers), it's possible to get a well-balanced and even sound.

Once the alley-oop technique is working, you should be able to watch the top of your hand throw down the first stroke and then the fingers "slam dunk" the second stroke. Remember that unless you're playing at medium-fast tempos and above, all of the notes are played as free strokes. The stick should resonate freely with a high pitch as it rebounds back up on its own. Keep the hand relaxed.

Alley-Oop Technique in Traditional Grip

Once the alley-oop technique is mastered with matched grip, it's time to look at how to employ the same technique using traditional grip (if desired). The first free stroke should be played with a rotation of the wrist, and the second free stroke should be played using mainly the thumb and first two fingers on top of the stick. Remember that with free strokes in traditional grip, it's important not to hold the stick against the ring finger. That tighter position would take away the opportunity to "oop" the second stroke, since the stick would be locked on the brakes the entire time.

Play the second stroke with higher velocity than the first by incorporating the thumb and top fingers. Once the traditional-grip alley-oop technique is working, you should be able to watch your hand rotate on the first stroke and then the top-side fingers and thumb "slam dunk" the second stroke. Unless you're playing so fast that the second stroke needs to be played as a downstroke, both beats of the alley-oop should be played as relaxed free strokes.

Alley-Oop Stroke Types: Free/Free Versus Free/Down

Alley-oop doubles can be played as two free strokes or as a free stroke and a downstroke where the stick stops close to the drum. Both methods are viable, but there are times when one or the other is preferable due to physical demands or musical application. At slow and medium-slow tempos, the second stroke should be a free stroke that's played more by the fingers than the wrists. Playing both strokes as free strokes works in this tempo range because there's time for the stick to float back up after the diddle.

At medium-fast tempos and above, the second stroke will need to become a downstroke. In this tempo range, there isn't enough time for the fingers to open and allow the stick to float up after either stroke. Instead, the rebound of the first stroke pushes the fingers open, and then the fingers grab the stick into the palm, which accelerates the stick and adds the necessary velocity so that the volume of the second stroke matches that of the first stroke. This technique also makes the second stroke a downstroke.

You'll get a bigger, smoother, and rounder sound with less effort if you work up the finesse required to play doubles as free/free strokes at applicable tempos. Unless they're desired for musical effect or they're required because you're playing on a mushy playing surface (like a floor tom), try to avoid playing doubles as a free stroke/downstroke combination, because the second notes can sound forced, stiff, and choked.

Fast Alley-Oop Doubles

When playing faster double-stroke rolls (roughly 32nd notes at 90 bpm and up), the alley-oop technique must be modified in order to prevent wrist strain. At this point, the forearms will be added to provide relief. When the rolls get very fast (roughly 32nd notes at 130 bpm and up), the wrists aren't really used much at all, and the alley-oop becomes forearm and fingers rather than wrist and fingers.

It's helpful to play fast rolls with an "on top of the stick" posture, where the wrists point downward slightly, relative to the forearm, and the sticks point down toward the drum at a steeper angle. This posture gives you more leverage to push into the drum as your forearms pump to play the first note and the front two fingers accelerate the second. (At very high speeds, it's unrealistic for the back two fingers to move far and quickly enough to maintain contact with the stick.)

Triple Strokes: Alley-Oop-Oop

When applying the alley-oop technique to triple strokes, simply add a third stroke played mainly from the fingers. The first note should be made mostly with the wrist, and the second and third strokes should be made mainly with the fingers (though the wrist does move a bit). The stick will naturally drop down with each stroke, but if you play the second and third strokes with greater and greater velocity (from the fingers), it's possible to get a well-balanced, even sound.

At slow to medium tempos, your hands should be completely relaxed after throwing down the third stroke so that the stick can rebound on its own. At fast tempos, the free/free/downstroke combination will need to be used. No arm motion is necessary because there's plenty of time for the hand to reset without any strain.

Developing the Alley-Oop Technique

Don't overanalyze and exaggerate the wrist/finger motion in the alley-oop and alley-oop-oop techniques. Practice the motion slowly so that it's more like two or three free strokes played from the wrist. As you gradually increase the speed, the fingers will automatically start to kick in on the second and third strokes.

To develop the all-important finger control required in the alley-oop and alley-oop-oop techniques, practice as many repetitions as possible, making sure that the last stroke in the double or triple is played as a true free stroke and rebounds all the way back up on its own. If you practice faster than a tempo at which you can accomplish this correctly, then you're not developing the correct technique.

Try not to squeeze the stick with the front two fingers to control the bounce, but instead focus on building finger control so that even at very fast tempos you can still use the front two fingers to punch the rebound strokes with extra velocity.

After focusing on the free/free method for alley-oop doubles, I recommend also building up the free stroke/downstroke approach where you accent the second beat of the double as a downstroke, with extra velocity from the fingers. I find it preferable to invert the roll (RLLR or LRRL) so that the accented second notes land on the downbeats rather than on the upbeats.

Troubleshooting Your Diddles

There are four common mistakes that many drummers make when playing alley-oops.

1. Weak, bouncing diddles. If your fingers are underdeveloped, the secondary beats will sound weak compared with the first stroke. Go slowly, and focus on the second stroke being a powerful free stroke that rebounds all the way back up.

2. Tight diddles played with all wrist and no fingers. While it's possible to play diddles at slow tempos using just the wrist, you'll run into trouble at medium and fast tempos. The fingers need to play the stick instead of gripping it against the brakes. Go slowly and focus on both notes of the diddles being played as free strokes that rebound back up.

3. Picking up the second stroke. If you have to pick up the second stroke, you're playing it as a downstroke rather than a loose free stroke. The extra tension needed to stop the stick and then pick it up robs you of flow and sound quality. Make sure the second stroke is a true free stroke that rebounds back up on its own. (Note: At higher speeds where the forearm is added, it's okay to break this rule.)

4. Tight hands at fast tempos. When playing doubles at fast tempos, the forearms need to be added into the motion in order to relieve the wrists. It's also helpful to back off the velocity of the first stroke a bit so that you have a better chance to get the volume of the second stroke to match that of the first.

DOWNSTROKES, TAPS, AND UPSTROKES

If we used only free strokes, our playing would become pretty dull, since every note would be played at the same stick height and dynamic level. In order to add accents and dynamic contour to the music, you'll need to modify the free stroke into downstrokes and upstrokes.

The downstroke starts high and stops down close to the head. This stroke is used to transition from an accent to a tap. The upstroke starts low and ends high and is used to transition from a tap to an accent. It's important to understand that the free stroke is the foundation for both downstrokes and upstrokes. The more control of downstrokes and upstrokes you have, the more dynamic your music will become.

Downstrokes in Matched Grip

First let's look at the downstroke in matched grip. The downstroke is also commonly referred to as a "staccato" stroke. *Staccato* is the musical term meaning short and seperated, which in this case refers to the accent's hand motion being short and seperated from the following taps. The downstroke is just like the free stroke until a split second after you hit the drum, when the stick should be squeezed against the palm of the hand (the brakes) in order to absorb the stick's energy and stop it low to the drum for a following tap. Squelching the stick's rebound against the brakes will have a little bit of physical impact, and it will cut off some of the stick's resonance. This is okay. Just be sure to avoid staying on the brakes the entire time you play the downstroke. At the top of the stroke, the butt end of the stick should be off the palm so that the stick is loose in the hand and the wrist and fingers have the opportunity to accelerate the stick toward the drum. Keeping the stick against the palm the entire time is like driving with one foot on the gas and one foot on the brake and will result in a tight, stiff, and ultimately slower stroke.

It's helpful to think about the following statement when playing downstrokes: *Downstrokes point down*. This posture gives you some leverage, which is helpful in quickly squelching the stick's rebound. In order for the downstroke to point down, you must play on top of the stick so that the fulcrum is held higher than the bead of the stick. This puts the hand in a position where immediately after gripping the stick against the palm, the wrist can drop down in order for the fingers to open up and freely play the stick. (Playing on top of the stick will also help avoid accidental rimshots when playing downstrokes.)

It's crucial that the thumb is located a bit on the topside of the stick so that it's in a good position to push down against the stick's natural rebound. The challenge is to develop the ability to hit the brakes quickly and then quickly release the brakes so that your fingers are ready to loosely play the next stroke.

Downstrokes in Traditional Grip

Once downstrokes are mastered with matched grip, it's time to look at using the same technique with traditional grip (if desired). To play the downstroke, start with a free stroke where the wrist rotates and the thumb and topside fingers accelerate the stick toward the drum. Remember to avoid holding the stick against the ring finger, since the ring finger (and pinkie underneath) functions as the brakes in traditional grip.

With the hand held loosely, accelerate the stick toward the drum with high velocity. Immediately after striking the head, quickly hit the brakes by squeezing the stick with the thumb and first two fingers against the cuticle of the ring finger. The faster you can stop the stick and then release it, the sooner the hand is prepared to get a fresh start playing the following relaxed and flowing tap strokes.

Taps and Upstrokes

Taps are very simple once you've mastered the free stroke, since they're nothing more than low free strokes. When playing taps, avoid squeezing the stick against the brakes. The stick should feel heavy, and it should resonate freely.

The upstroke is also very simple. It starts as a tap stroke (or low free stroke), but immediately after you hit the drum you lift up the stick in preparation for an accent. Avoid squeezing the stick against the brakes while playing the stroke and while lifting the stick. You want the fingers to be in an open position at the top of the upstroke so they're prepared to help accelerate the stick for the following stroke. Other than the split second when the fingers squeeze the stick during a downstroke, you always want the fingers to help play the stick and not grip the stick.

Putting It All Together: Full, Down, Up, and Tap Strokes

To play patterns with accents and taps you'll need to use all four basic strokes (full, down, up, and tap). The full stroke is a high stroke that starts and ends high. (Full strokes are the same as free strokes and should be played where the stick is allowed to rebound back up on it's own.) The downstroke is a high stroke that ends low. The upstroke is a low stroke that ends high. The tap stroke is a low stroke that stays low. (Tap strokes should be played as low free strokes with relaxed hands and without squeezing the stick against the palm.)

The stroke type you use within a given rhythm or rudiment is determined by the stroke height of the following note played by the same hand. Downstrokes and upstrokes should be used when the following stroke is played at a new stick height. When there is no change in stick height for the following note, the free stroke should be used (at the full- or tap-stroke height). The goal is to play free strokes as often as possible in order to play as loosely as possible. Play downstrokes only when necessary.

Here's another way of looking at it: Every stroke within an accent/tap pattern will be played smoothly and relaxed, and the butt end of the stick will never get squeezed against the brakes, with the exception of the downstrokes. Aside from the times when you need to use downstrokes, every other stroke should remain relaxed and flowing so that the stick feels heavy and resonates freely in a loosely held hand.

Developing Downstrokes, Taps, and Upstrokes

I don't recommend playing downstrokes before mastering the free stroke, since the free stroke is your foundation. If you start playing advanced vocabulary containing various accents and taps before you've mastered the free stroke, you could end up with a tight grip that will take a long time to remedy.

The best exercise to develop accent/tap control is the Ultimate Accent/Tap exercise found on page 74. When practicing those exercises, maximize the contrast between the stick heights of the accents and the taps, and remember that the downstrokes should point down. The taps should be played at 4" heights. At the top of the tap stroke, the stick is about parallel to the drum. (It may help to make a cardboard 4" height guide and tape it to your drum or practice pad to check yourself.)

Listen to every tap for even, consistent sound quality. No tap should be louder or softer than any other tap, and no accent should be louder or softer than any other accent. The goal is to develop complete control over very high accents and very low taps so that ultimately you can decide what stick heights you want to use in a given musical situation.

Rhythmic accuracy is also extremely important while you're training yourself to perform these key hand motions. Set your metronome to play the smallest subdivisions you're practicing, and try to bury the metronome, which means you're so locked in that you don't hear the clicks.

With straight 8th-note exercises, I recommend starting at 100 bpm and going up in ten-beat increments.

Troubleshooting Accents and Taps

There are three common errors to avoid when playing accent/tap patterns.

1. Downstrokes are played too tightly. Avoid squeezing the stick against the brakes while playing the stroke (you want to squelch the rebound only *after* the stick has struck the drum), and avoid trying to "dig in" or hit the drum extra-hard. This common mistake robs you of smooth sound quality, flow, speed, and endurance, and it can lead to injury, since the extra tension causes all the shock of hitting the drum to go directly into your hands.

2. When playing taps after a downstroke, the stick is held with the butt end squeezed against the brakes. This also creates extra tension and robs you of smooth sound quality, flow, speed, and endurance, and it can lead to injury.

3. The downstroke lacks control, so the stick flops somewhat out of control into the following taps. While error number three is certainly favorable to errors one and two, this error leads to high, bouncy taps that lack dynamic contrast relative to the accents. Check that the thumb is on the topside of the stick where it can push down. There shouldn't be a gap between the thumb and first finger, and you should be playing on top of the stick for leverage. Rhythmic accuracy is often sacrificed as well. (At fast speeds where there isn't enough time to stop the stick after the stroke, some flop can be useful. But you have to learn the rules before you can break them!)

MOELLER WHIP STROKE AND MOELLER WHIP-STROKE COMBINATION

The Moeller whip stroke is named after Sanford "Gus" Moeller, a famous teacher from the early 1900s who became known for teaching a whipping motion used by Civil War drummers. In recent years, "Moeller" has become a buzzword for good technique, and many have turned it into an elusive mystery.

A Moeller stroke is simply a whip stroke, used for accents, played from the forearm instead of the wrist, but the "Moeller technique" (or "Moeller method") is an approach involving a whipped accent followed by freely rebounding taps. To delineate the two techniques, I'll refer to them as the "Moeller whip stroke" and the "Moeller whip-stroke combination."

When using the Moeller whip stroke, the forearm lifts up the hand, which hangs limp, and then the stick is whipped down in order to achieve the accent. The forearm drags the hand and stick up and down, so the forearm is always the first thing to move and the stick is always the last thing to move. It may be helpful to think about playing the stroke with the palm of the hand (or the end of the forearm) while letting the hand and stick naturally find their way to the drum slightly after the fact.

The Moeller whip downstroke, or what I call the "whip-and-stop," should be used when there's time to stop the stick low after the accent preceding the next low tap. The Moeller whip-stroke combination (whip-and-flop) should be used when there's a tap immediately following the accent and you want to flow into it, or where a smooth and effortless flow is desired over maximum dynamic contrast. Either way, the Moeller whip approach should be applied when playing accent/tap rudiments and patterns at high speeds in order to prevent the wrists from tightening up.

Moeller Whip Stroke in Matched Grip

To play a full-size Moeller whip stroke in matched grip, hold the sticks in the American or German position so that the butt end pokes out to the side of the hand. (Moeller will also work in French grip, but only with a much smaller motion due to the wrist's limited side-to-side range of motion.)

You may also want to use the second-finger fulcrum instead of the first-finger fulcrum, since more of the energy of the whip will transfer to the stick when you hold it with the second finger, and you won't need intricate finger finesse when applying this technique.

Hold on to the stick with your fulcrum just tight enough that you don't drop the stick. Starting with the sticks near the drum, let the wrist relax as you pick up the entire arm from the shoulder. (It may help to think about the upper arm dragging up the forearm, hand, and stick.) At this

point the hand and stick should be dangling and pointing down toward the drum. While keeping the wrist totally relaxed, throw the arm down. In the blink of an eye, the arm passes the hand and stick, and the hand and stick are now pointing up relative to the forearm. At this point, the hand is whipped toward the drum faster than the forearm, and the stick is whipped toward the drum faster than the hand. *Boom!*

After striking the drum, you can either stop the stick near the head (downstroke) or let it rebound back up by opening the fingers. Either way, it's important that you don't lift the forearm back up immediately after the Moeller whip stroke. The arm should stay down and relax.

As the tempo increases, the size of the Moeller whip-stroke motion will need to decrease.

This is why the Moeller whip stroke is more commonly played from the forearm and not the upper arm. As the speed increases even more, the motion should continue to decrease. At very high speeds, the Moeller whip stroke will look like nothing more than a twitch of the wrist, which is actually the forearm throwing down slightly in order to make the hand and stick rise relative to the forearm. At this point, there's also the effect of the palm bumping down the butt end of the stick in order to pop up the front end.

A pure Moeller whip stroke doesn't engage the wrist muscles. It's impossible for the wrist to throw down at the speed of the whip, so engaging the muscles that control the wrist will just slow down the stroke, add tension, and defeat the whipping motion.

Moeller Whip Stroke in Traditional Grip

Once the Moeller whip stroke is mastered with matched grip, it's time to practice it using traditional grip (if desired). In traditional grip, the left-hand stick is now whipped around the forearm as the radius and ulna bones rotate.

Starting with the stick close to the drum, lift the upper arm away from the body while allowing the forearm, hand, and stick to relax and hang freely. At this point, the stick should be hanging with the tip pointing down toward the floor or even pointing slightly away from the body.

To start the whip stroke, pull the upper arm in toward your body. This will leave the forearm, hand, and stick to twist around and point toward the ceiling for a split second before they are whipped toward the drum. In the blink of an eye, the forearm is whipped faster than the upper arm, the hand is whipped faster than the forearm, and the stick is whipped faster than the hand. Remember that from the elbow down, the arm must be completely relaxed, or muscle tension will cancel out the speed generated through the whip.

As with Moeller whip strokes in matched grip, as the speed increases, the motion of the stroke will need to decrease.

The traditional-grip Moeller whip stroke is more commonly played using the forearm, with much less exaggerated upper-arm movement. As the speed increases even more, the motion should decrease to the point where the Moeller whip stroke looks like nothing more than a twitch of the wrist (which is actually the forearm throwing down slightly, relative to the hand).

Moeller Upstroke

When a low tap immediately precedes an accent and you want to use the Moeller whip technique, you'll need to play a Moeller upstroke. Think of this as a preparation stroke used to set up the Moeller whip-stroke accent. Here, the stick works like a seesaw. As the back of the stick gets picked up, the front drops down and plays an incidental tap. Don't intentionally play the upstroke by engaging the wrist or fingers. It may be helpful to think of dragging the hand and stick up away from the drum with the forearm as the stroke is played. Also, don't lift the arm prior to playing this tap, because then you would have to engage your wrist muscles in order to play the tap. (This is the most common mistake made when learning Moeller upstrokes.)

The Moeller upstroke should just drop in and hit the drum as a droopy tap. Feel the forearm lift and the wrist drop down (like a dog paw) at the same time as the tap is played incidentally (the seesaw effect). If it feels lazy and out of control, you're probably doing it right. With practice, you'll develop enough finesse to ensure that these incidental taps hit the drum with rhythmic accuracy.

Moeller Whip-Stroke Combination (Whip-and-Flop Technique)

When drummers speak of the Moeller technique or the Moeller method, they're often talking about a system of applying the Moeller whip stroke within groups of accents and taps. The idea is to start with a Moeller whip stroke and then let the stick rebound freely into one or more bounce taps before repeating the cycle. No physical work is involved in playing the taps. The constant motion of this whip-and-flop technique takes stress off the body.

It may help to look at the Moeller whip-stroke combination in this manner: Your forearm drags the hand and stick up and down, while lazy bounce taps drop in between the accents.

The Moeller whip-stroke combination is most often used when playing consecutive sets of two notes (accent, tap), three notes (accent, tap, tap), or four notes (accent, tap, tap, tap) with the same hand. The accents are all played as Moeller whip strokes, and the taps in the middle are bounces. The last tap preceding the next accent is a Moeller upstroke. The goal is to get two or more strokes from one whipping motion. (As you get into groupings of four notes and higher, finger control will start to become necessary to keep the taps going, since the accent's energy will gradually dissipate.)

The forearms pick up the stick for the Moeller upstroke only on the very last tap preceding the accent. If you lift the arms prior to that, the rebound potential of the inner taps is reduced, the sound of the taps changes, and the velocity of the upcoming Moeller whip stroke is preemptively slowed down.

With the Moeller whip-stroke combination, you'll need to sacrifice the height accuracy of the low taps in order to maximize flow. The volume contrast between the accents and taps is now determined almost exclusively by the velocity of the strokes. The whip stroke is much faster than the taps and will therefore be louder than the following bounce-stroke taps.

You want to put the smoothness and flow of the Moeller whip-stroke combination ahead of the bigness of the accents. Don't punch the accents too hard, or else you'll have to hit the brakes in order to keep the next tap from coming in too early.

Developing the Moeller Whip Stroke and the Moeller Whip-Stroke Combination

I recommend working on the Moeller method *after* mastering the basic wrist-stroke techniques (free stroke, downstroke, and upstroke). The wrist strokes are the fundamentals, while the Moeller method falls in the category of "break the rules after you've learned them." While the Moeller method lends itself to a relaxed and flowing behind-the-beat feel, you should also have good wrist-stroke technique, since both approaches have their advantages and disadvantages.

Moeller whip strokes should first be learned as big, full motions starting from the shoulder. This allows you to fully understand the magnitude of the power available with this stroke. The size of the motion should be reduced as the tempo increases.

It's also beneficial to practice the motion without sticks in order to make sure that the hand is held limp and is relaxed. (See photos at top right.)

After getting the feel of the motion without sticks, add a stick between your thumb and second finger (or between your thumb and first finger in traditional grip). Use just enough pressure so as not to drop the stick. Continue to practice the motion with and without the stick until your

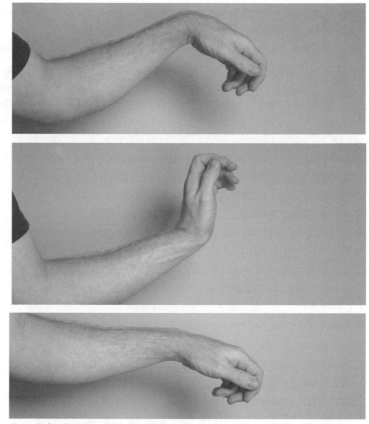

hand feels about the same either way. Remember that any use of the muscles that control the wrist will kill the whip.

For some exercises that use Moeller downstrokes, go to the inverted sticking patterns on page 82. To develop the Moeller whip-stroke combination, go to the Chops Builders exercises on page 55. Start by practicing them slowly at tempos where they could otherwise be played with basic wrist-stroke techniques. It's important to practice the Moeller whip motion slowly in order to develop the necessary muscle memory.

Troubleshooting the Moeller Method

There are three common errors to avoid when playing Moeller whip strokes and Moeller whip-stroke combinations.

1. Using the wrist. Most drummers are so used to using the wrist to play strokes that it feels weird to let the hand flop while the arm takes over. When starting a Moeller stroke, check that the end of your forearm comes up first and the hand and stick trail behind. The bead of the stick should be the *last* thing to rise.

2. Picking up the arm immediately after hitting the accent and before the following tap. When this happens, you're forced to engage your wrist muscles to play a tap after the accent. With the arm staying down, the taps should simply bounce and drop in with no extra effort.

3. Picking up the forearm before the final tap. Pick up the arm to play the Moeller upstroke only on the last tap preceding the accent. Otherwise the sound quality and rebound of the taps will decrease, and the following Moeller accent will have less power, since the preparation on the way up is so slow.

PERFECT PRACTICE AND BUILDING SPEED

Many drum instructors say, "Play naturally." The problem with that statement is that we naturally hold on to things tightly. Have you ever seen someone pick up a drumstick for the first time and play smooth rebounding strokes? Great technique is rarely natural, but once it's achieved, this newfound finesse looks very natural, since we're using our body in the most efficient way possible. There's almost always a technique that will make what you're trying to do much easier, and developing that technique takes time, but it's time well spent.

The goal of your practice sessions should be to become a great musical drummer with a wide range of technical abilities and a large rhythmic vocabulary. Many drummers practice for long periods of time, but many of them also practice incorrectly. Perfect practice makes perfect, while imperfect practice cements bad habits that will be difficult to overcome later and can sometimes lead to injury. If you're getting injured from drumming, chances are you're doing something wrong and you're asking too much of your body.

Drumming should not hurt. A little bit of muscle burn is to be expected when developing any new or underdeveloped technique, because the muscles will be learning new movements. But anything beyond that is dangerous. Practice these new motions with plenty of breaks to let the muscles build up gradually.

Perfect Practice Equipment

Sticks: A bigger stick will rebound a bit more. (Compare the rebound potential of a 2B with that of a 7A.) It will be much more difficult to develop finger control with a stick that's less inclined to rebound on its own. I recommend practicing with medium-size and larger drumsticks.

Practice pads: While I love my Vic Firth Heavy Hitter Stockpad for general use, it's also good to occasionally practice on everything from countertops to pillows. The drumset has many surfaces that feel very different. A countertop feels a bit like a hi-hat, while a pillow feels a bit like a loosely tuned floor tom. Of course, spending a lot of practice time playing on a pillow or a mushy-feeling pad with little rebound won't allow you to develop finger control, since you'll always have to pick up the sticks on your own. Without well-developed finger control, you'll be left without much finesse and will have major technical limitations. Practicing mostly on a drum pad with good rebound will leave you with well-trained hands that can execute ideas on just about any playing surface.

Metronome: Without a metronome (or music to play along with when you don't need a specific tempo or subdivision), you'll likely be practicing incorrectly and cementing bad habits. The metronome is always in time, and you want to train your perception of accurate time accordingly. Pretend that the metronome is a fellow musician that you want to lock in with. Bury every beat from the metronome so that it sounds as if you're triggering it from your pad or drum. Aside from doing wonders for your timing, this approach will help develop your ears for locking in with other musicians. Think about this: However uncomfortable or frustrating the metronome is for you to play with, that's how uncomfortable and frustrating you are for other musicians to play with and for the audience to listen to. Create good habits by consistently practicing with a metronome or recorded music.

Isolation headphones: Drums are loud, and repeated exposure to such high sound-pressure levels can damage your ears. Young drummers often feel invincible, but the beating you're putting on your ears now will come back to haunt you later. There are many brands of isolation headphones and in-ear monitors that protect your ears while allowing you to hear your metronome or music. Be smart and protect yourself.

Audio recorder: There's a huge difference between first-person and third-person perception, and a recorder will help you hear yourself more clearly. When you're playing (first person), you may perceive what you're doing as being accurate. When you listen back to a recording of yourself (third person), it's often a completely different story. While it can be scary to face the truth, listening back to yourself is one of the most important things you can do to improve. Even the cheapest audio recorder you can find will serve you well.

You and your body: You can get in a lot of chops practice without having sticks in your hands. Putting your forearms flat on a surface and drumming with your hands can give you a great wrist workout. The same works for your feet. Keep the heels flat on the ground and tap the balls of your feet on the floor. Even if you play your bass drum using a heels-up technique, you'll still get a great ankle workout by practicing this way.

Find an Excellent Teacher

I can't stress enough how important it is to find a qualified private instructor. Reading books, watching videos, and researching technical information online is beneficial, but actually applying those concepts correctly is another matter. Even after studying and watching videos on technique, most people practice and play some things incorrectly, so they never realize their full potential. Find a teacher who can explain how and why to play a certain way so that you'll have incentive to practice and improve on your weaknesses. When I teach hand technique, I always make sure students see their deficiencies and understand why their approach isn't working nearly as well as the more correct approach. Sometimes it takes an outside perspective to make the light bulb go on so you can play using the most appropriate approach.

Developing Muscle Memory

Developing proper muscle memory for drumming is crucial, since it will allow you to play correctly without having to think about technique. Muscle memory is what allows you to perform a physical task without thinking about it, such as tying your shoes. Developing muscle memory requires a lot of repetitions—some say as many as 3,000 to 5,000. For drumming, we want to make sure that our repetitions are correct in order to develop the correct muscle memory. Incorrect practice forms bad habits that will take even longer to reprogram. This is why I recommend practicing no faster than you play correctly and comfortably, or else you're developing incorrect and/or uncomfortable muscle memory.

Developing Coordination

When you're first learning new vocabulary, don't practice any faster than the tempo that allows you enough time to initiate a stroke within the smallest rhythmic subdivision (like 16th notes). In the beginning, your mind needs time to think about what's next before reaching the tempo where preparatory motions, like upstrokes, need to be performed while the other hand is still playing.

Once you're comfortable playing something very slowly, stay at that tempo for a few minutes. Then speed it up to the tempo that requires one hand to prep while the other hand is playing. To build the maximum rhythmic accuracy when practicing slowly, set your metronome so that it plays as many rhythmic subdivisions as is appropriate for what you're playing.

Building Speed

Let me start with a disclaimer: Speed is worthless if it's not used musically. That said, it's always good to have the ability to play something really fast when the perfect musical opportunity comes around. Having more than enough ability is always a good thing, as the more abilities you have, the more options you'll have to draw from when the time is right.

While many drummers seem to think that playing fast is difficult, it's typically not that much different from playing at any other tempo. More often than not, it's just a matter of adjusting your approach. High-speed drumming requires three things: lower stick heights, a lighter touch into the drum, and a change in technique. It's all a matter of figuring out how to do less work, since an increase in speed requires a decrease in motion.

Most people have technique barriers that stop them from reaching faster speeds, but these can be overcome by correctly practicing the techniques necessary to play at the faster speeds. The key is to practice the faster tempo's technique slowly in order to develop it at a comfortable pace.

To work up speed on any rudiment or pattern, practice many perfect repetitions playing along with a metronome or music at a comfortable tempo. Watch your stick heights and match the ratio of wrist-to-finger usage in each hand. Don't go any faster than the top speed at which it's easy to play perfectly and comfortably (which will most likely be very slow at first).

Even though it's not very challenging, stay at a comfortable tempo for as long as twenty minutes. Then bump up the tempo about ten beats per minute and repeat the process. Do this daily for a couple weeks to cement the muscle memory. You will get much faster in less time by taking this more patient approach. When drummers practice at the edge of how fast as they can go, they're almost always doing so at the expense of proper technique. Plus they're developing improper muscle memory that will be difficult to unlearn and reprogram later.

Summing Up

The more time you can allot to practice, the better. Just make sure that, regardless of how much (or how little) time you spend on these exercises, you spend the time practicing *effectively*. Spend the majority of your practice time focusing on your weaknesses. I encourage you to extrapolate any minute pattern from any of the exercises and isolate it for as long as it takes to perfect. Try to keep your practice time as fun as possible by playing along with music that you like or by creating a challenging game, like trying to play something perfectly five times in a row before bumping up the tempo.

There will be off days when your body just doesn't perform at its highest level, but remember that all practice repetitions help build you up as long as they're performed correctly. You'll be getting better with each practice session, even if the results aren't readily apparent.

The bottom line is that there are no shortcuts to building great technique. Your hands need thousands of correct repetitions more than anything else. As for applying your newly developed hand technique to the drumset, don't over-think it. The techniques will transfer to your drumset playing automatically, since you've spent the time learning the optimal techniques for a given motion. At the end of the day, you want to have more than enough chops at your disposal so your mind is free to focus on more important things—like music!

INTRODUCTION

The rudiments are the roots of our drumming art form and are every bit as important today as they were when they were created. I think of the rudiments as the alphabet of our drumming language. Once you've learned this alphabet, you're ready to use it to freely express yourself with a large vocabulary. I've heard drummers say that rudiments and techniques will stiffen them up, ruin their groove, and confine their imagination. This couldn't be farther from the truth, assuming that the rudiments are learned in a musical way and are played with smooth and flowing technique.

When it comes to drumset applications, too often drummers just focus on how to orchestrate a given rudiment around the instrument. While this approach is of value, I don't think it offers enough incentive to make you want to take the time to properly master the rudiments.

For drumset players, the real value of rudiments lies in the physical motions and techniques that are built up and can then be applied in other contexts. While there are many rudiments out there, from the Percussive Arts Society's standard forty to a seemingly endless array of hybrids, I've distilled the list down to the twelve rudiments that contain the essential hand motions you'll need to master in order to play any other rudiment or sticking pattern. Let's look at them one at a time.

1. **Single-stroke roll.** This rudiment covers successive identical free strokes.
2. **Double-stroke roll.** This two-stroke combination requires finger control for the second stroke (alley-oop) and the use of pumping forearms at fast tempos.
3. **Triple-stroke roll.** This three-stroke combination requires finger control for the second and third strokes (alley-oop-oop).
4. **Buzz roll.** This rudiment requires fulcrum/hand pressure into the drumhead.
5. **Paradiddle.** This rudiment involves downstrokes and upstrokes, plus a low double after an accent (alley-opp or drop-catch motion).
6. **Six-stroke roll.** This rudiment contains accents within a roll motion where the wrists turn for accents while the forearms continue pumping, as well as downstrokes and upstrokes.
7. **Flam.** This rudiment contains downstrokes and upstrokes, as well as the Moeller whip-stroke combination (whip-and-flop) at faster tempos.
8. **Flam accent.** This rudiment includes downstrokes and upstrokes, plus a low triple stroke (drop-dribble-catch) after an accent.
9. **Flam tap.** This rudiment contains a bouncing, decrescendoing triple-stroke motion (no-chop flop-and-drop) at medium and fast tempos.
10. **Inverted flam tap.** This rudiment includes the Moeller whip downstroke (whip-and-stop).
11. **Drag.** This rudiment covers finger control rebound into finger control double strokes (at faster tempos).
12. **Dragadiddle.** This rudiment includes accented doubles played with the free stroke/downstroke combination (dribble-catch).

Once you have command of these twelve rudiments, then you can easily work out the coordination to play just about anything else. Rudiments create chops, chops create vocabulary, and vocabulary creates music.

RUDIMENTAL BREAKDOWN

The rudimental breakdown is the process of playing a rudiment from slow to fast to slow as evenly as possible over one minute. It's also been called the open-closed-open breakdown. To alleviate any confusion, "open-closed-open" does not mean to go from an open double-stroke roll to a closed buzz roll. The rudiment itself should never change. In the breakdown, the rudiment should be sped up for twenty-five seconds, held for ten seconds, and then slowed down for twenty-five seconds. You want to focus on evenness and consistent sound quality throughout the process.

Since rudiments require different techniques at different tempos, the rudimental breakdown is the truest test of mastery. Not only are you covering every possible tempo, but you're also demonstrating your ability to transfer from one technique to the next in correlation with the gradual tempo change. The breakdown will also show you the tempos at which you are deficient, so you will know what tempos you need to practice in order to fully master the rudiment. Once you can go through the breakdown with each rudiment and achieve good sound quality and flow, you'll be ready to play the rudiment in any context you might encounter.

Here are some tips for the rudimental breakdown.

1. Do not rush through it. Use a stopwatch that shows the seconds to make sure you spend as much time slowing down the rudiment as you do speeding up the rudiment. (Slowing down is the more difficult part.)

2. Evenness and consistent sound quality are the most important things, not your top speed.

3. There should be no abrupt changes in tempo or in the velocity of your strokes. You want to morph between tempos and techniques in a smooth and gradual manner.

4. Don't sacrifice execution for faster speed.

5. Gradually lower and raise the stick heights during the breakdown. The change in stick height is so slight that it shouldn't be noticeable at any one point.

6. Rudiments with a single stick height (no accents) should start and stop with the sticks up.

7. Rudiments with two stick heights (containing accents) should start and stop with the sticks low to the drum.

Rick Malkin

SINGLE-STROKE ROLL

Playing rudiments properly is a challenge because they are so physically demanding—not so much in terms of muscular strength, but in terms of finesse and dexterity. Many repetitions are necessary in order to train your muscles and to develop the coordination required to play them effortlessly. But all of that practice will be time well spent, since once you develop the proper muscle memory you'll never have to think about the mechanics of the rudiment again.

The first rudiment we're going to look at is the single-stroke roll. The single-stroke roll should be played with free strokes (also known as full strokes or legato strokes), which means that the hands are holding the sticks loosely and are "dribbling" them on the drumhead. Resist any temptation to hold the sticks tightly or to stop the stick at the bottom of the stroke. Allow the stick to rebound back to the "up" position immediately after striking the head.

The technique needed to play this rudiment is pretty much the same at any speed, though different wrist-to-finger ratios will be required depending on the rebound (or lack thereof) of the playing surface. It's common for many players to favor the fingers at high speeds, but keep in mind that finger technique won't work very well on a relatively mushy surface like a floor tom head.

In addition to the exercises provided, be sure to practice this rudiment going evenly from slow to fast to slow over a one-minute period. Practice the exercises with the given stickings, use a metronome (or play along with your favorite tunes), and don't go any faster than you can play comfortably. Note for exercises 2 and 3: Whenever you see a one-bar repeat sign, play the previous measure using the opposite sticking, beginning with the left hand. The only exception to this is in the last measure of each example.

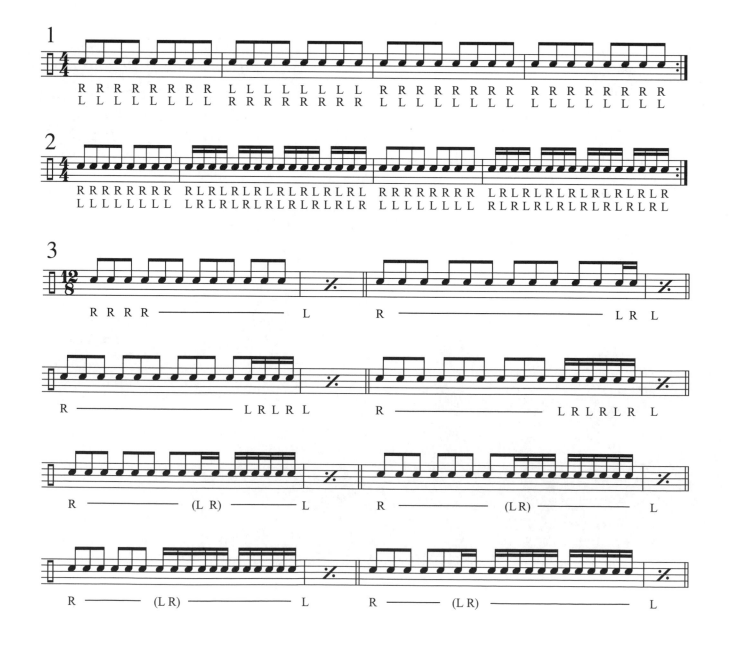

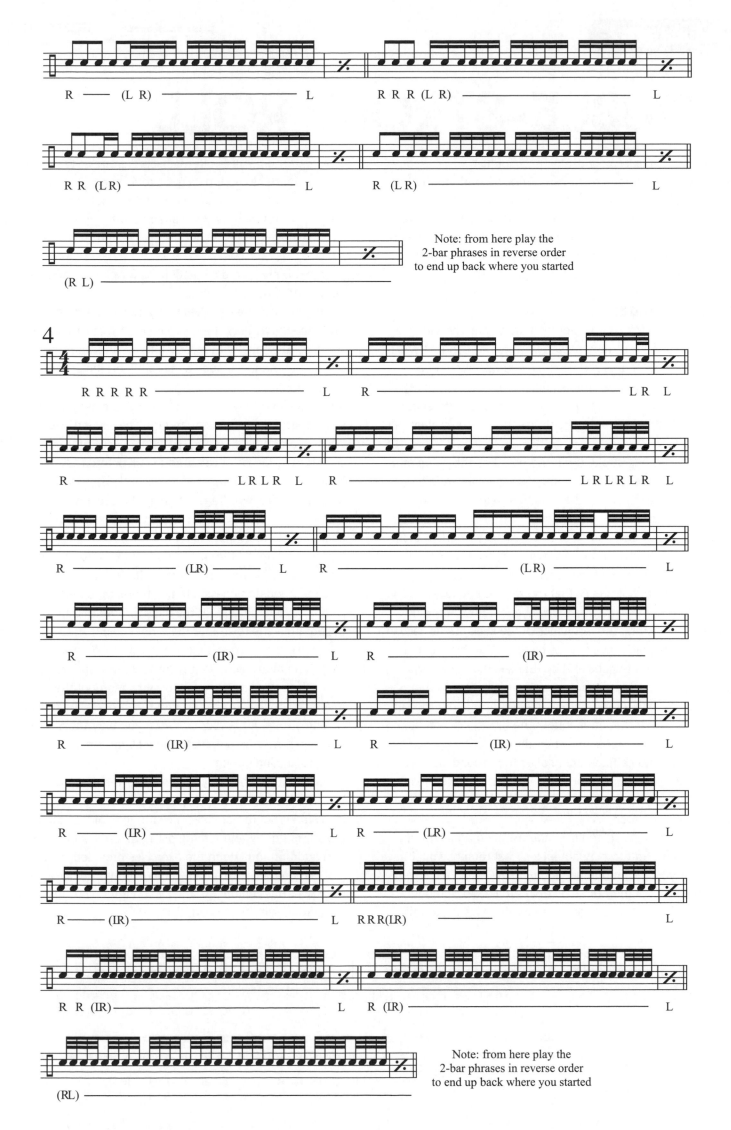

Note: from here play the
2-bar phrases in reverse order
to end up back where you started

Note: from here play the
2-bar phrases in reverse order
to end up back where you started

RRLLRRLL   RR   LL   RR   LL   R R L L R R L L
LLRRLLRR   LL   RR   LL   RR   L L R R L L R R

DOUBLE-STROKE ROLL

Doubles are extremely useful, and not just in a roll context. Isolated double strokes can be played around the drumset to produce musical effects or to give you a little extra time to prepare for your next drum or cymbal hit. In addition to those obvious applications, being able to play a good-quality double-stroke roll will likely improve your drumming in ways you wouldn't expect.

Define the Diddle

Proper double strokes (or "diddles") aren't simply bounced off the head. Nor are they played with two individual wrist strokes. At slow to medium tempos, doubles should be played as flowing free strokes (aka full or legato strokes) where the first stroke is played mainly with the wrist and the second is played mainly with the fingers (the "alley-oop" technique).

Think of the first stroke (with the wrist) as the setup and the second stroke (with the fingers) as the slam-dunk. Immediately after playing the second stroke, the hand should relax so that the stick rebounds to the "up" position by itself. (Remember that with free strokes you never pick up the stick, you only throw it down—just like dribbling a ball.) It's preferable to let the second stroke rebound up on its own because that proves that the second stroke was played with high velocity in a loose hand. Plus, there's no sense in dampening the resonance of the stick on the second stroke by clamping it against the palm if it can be avoided.

At medium-fast tempos and up, the second stroke will need to become a downstroke. In this tempo range there isn't enough time for the fingers to open and allow the stick to float up after either stroke. Now the first stroke's rebound pushes the fingers open, and then they react by grabbing the stick into the palm, which makes the second stroke a downstroke. (Pulling the stick into the palm accelerates the second stroke and adds the necessary velocity to match the first stroke's volume.)

Almost all rudiments require different techniques for different tempos, and to play doubles at fast tempos you'll have to change your technique yet again. Some amateur players push the limits of their double stroke–roll speed without adding forearms. The desired speed will never come this

way, and the result is often muscle tightness, which can lead to injury as the wrists get overworked. Regardless of the tempo, the technique used for the first note of a double will be determined by what's required to get the sound and dynamic level of the second note to match that of the first.

Here are my technical guidelines for playing double strokes at various tempos.

Slow: Play two free strokes using mostly wrist strokes.

Medium-Slow: Play the first stroke with mostly wrist and the second stroke with mostly fingers. Maintain the free stroke technique as much as possible on the second stroke of the diddle.

Medium-Fast: Play the first stroke with mostly wrist and the second stroke with mostly fingers. The second stroke will become a downstroke and the fingers accelerate the stroke during the process of catching the stick into the palm.

Fast: Play with forearms pumping (little or no wrist) and use mainly the first two fingers to play the second strokes. Make sure that you're playing on top of the stick for better leverage and that the thumb is on the topside of the stick (American grip) so that it can push down into the drum. There should be no gap between the thumb and first finger since that would necessitate much greater squeezing tension. The forearm will lift the stick in preparation for the next double stroke so that the wrist doesn't strain to do so.

Practice the following exercises using a metronome (or play them along with your favorite tunes), and don't go faster than you can play comfortably. Many of the exercises invert the double strokes so that the stronger beat is on the second stroke of the diddle. When you play these inverted phrases, it may be helpful to put a slight accent on each diddle's second stroke.

Keep in mind that as you push your technical limits, it's better to loosen up and play a bit weakly and bouncy than it is to stroke out the doubles. Be sure to avoid holding on to the sticks tightly and forcing out both strokes of the doubles.

In addition to playing the exercises provided, be sure to practice double-stroke rolls going evenly from slow to fast to slow over one minute, gradually changing your technique in correlation with the speed.

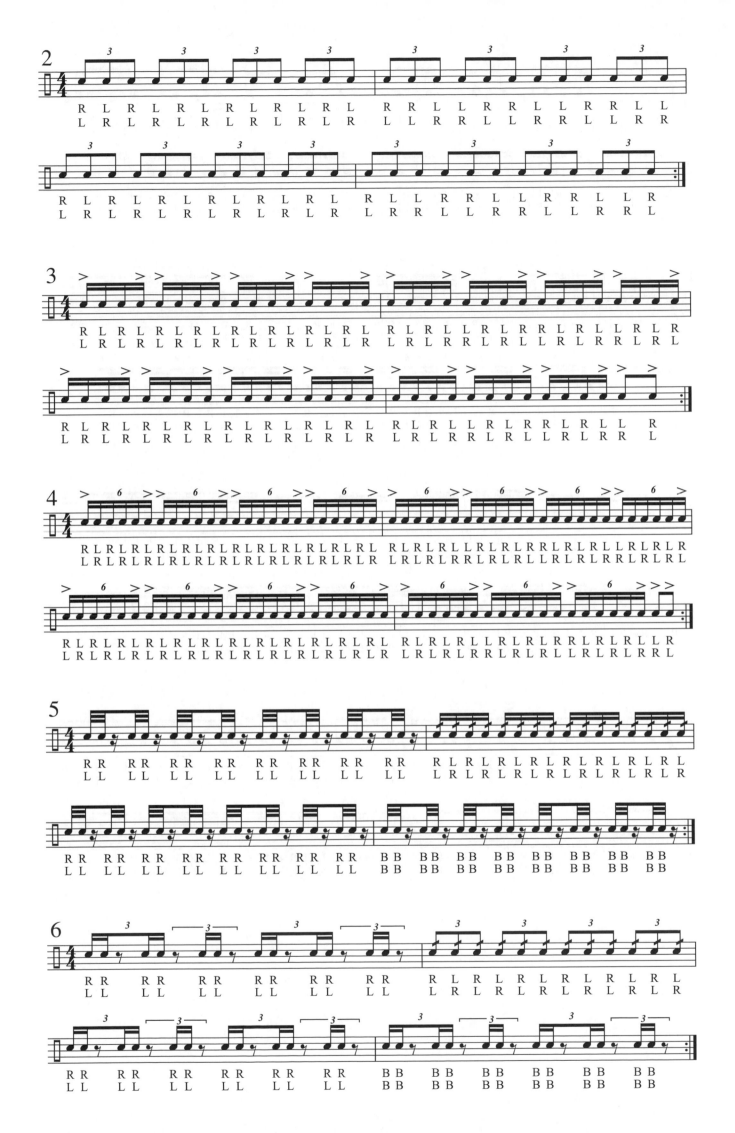

TRIPLE-STROKE ROLL

The triple-stroke roll, which is also known as "threes," is yet another crucial rudiment. Once you can play this rudiment well, you'll be armed with the ability to throw in isolated triple beats anywhere around the drumset.

Not many drummers play a complete two-handed triple-stroke roll on the kit. But triple strokes played by individual hands are pretty standard vocabulary. (For that matter, each hand actually plays a triple beat within a single-stroke sextuplet.)

Good-quality triple strokes are not simply bounced on the drumhead, nor is each stroke played individually with the wrist (unless you're playing threes very slowly). It's important to first develop a good double-stroke roll, since triple strokes are an extension of doubles. Threes should be played as flowing free strokes (aka full or legato strokes) where you never pick up the stick but only throw it down on the head like dribbling a ball. The first stroke should be played mainly with the wrist, while the second and third should be played mainly with the fingers (the "alley-oop-oop" technique). Think of the first stroke as the setup throw from the wrist and the second and third strokes as dribbles from the fingers. Immediately after playing the third stroke, the hand should relax so that the stick rebounds to the starting "up" position.

At faster tempos, the technique will change slightly. You'll have to pick up the stick after the third note when the increased speed makes it nearly impossible to play a free stroke. In this case, you will be a using a free-free-downstroke combination. The key is to use the fingers to add velocity to each individual stroke. When threes are played very fast, they will sound like a buzz roll. It's a little-known fact, but most buzz rolls are actually played using three strokes per hand.

For some players, threes may be easier to play by positioning the hands closer to a French grip (thumbs on top of the stick), because so much finger control is necessary to play the second and third beats. French grip favors the use of the fingers, while German grip (palms down) favors the wrist. When you play these exercises, experiment with different positions between French and German grip to find what works best for you. It's good to be comfortable with a bunch of hand positions, since different techniques will make certain patterns easier to play. Ultimately there is no "right" technique, and you want to be able to switch positions on the fly.

Practice the following exercises with a metronome (or play them along with your favorite tunes), and don't go any faster than you can play comfortably. Keep in mind that when the going gets tough it's always better to play a bit weakly and bouncy than it is to stroke out all three notes. Avoid holding on to the sticks too tightly and forcing out all three beats.

In addition to the exercises provided, be sure to practice the triple-stroke roll by going evenly from slow to fast to slow over one minute, gradually changing your technique in correlation with the speed.

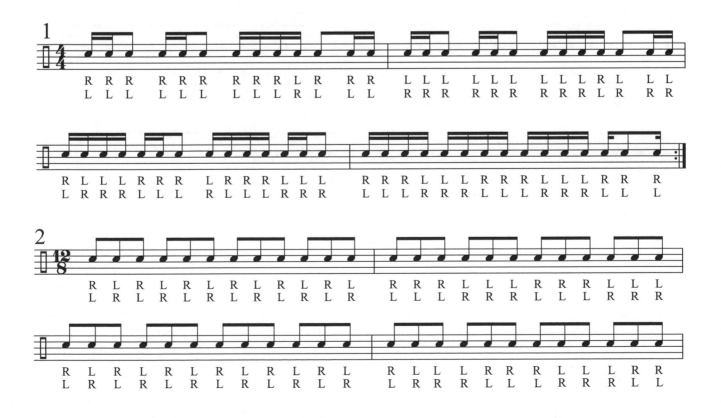

R L R L R L R L R L R L R L R L   R L R R R L L L R R L
L R L R L R L R L R L R L R L R   L R L L L R R R L L L R

3

R R R R R R R R R R R R L L L L L L L L L L L L R R
L L L L L L L L L L L L R R R R R R R R R R R R L L

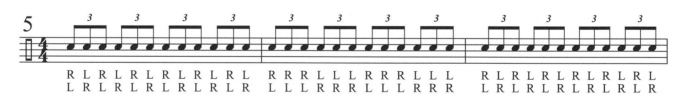

R R R R R R R R R R L L L L L L L L L L L L R R
L L L L L L L L L L R R R R R R R R R R R R L L

4

R L R L R R R L R R L   R L R L R L L L R L L L   R L R L R R R L L L R R R L
L R L R L L L R L L L R   L R L R L R R R L R R R   L R L R L L L R R R L L L R

5

R L R L R L R L R L R L   R R R L L L R R R L L L   R L R L R L R L R L R L
L R L R L R L R L R L R   L L L R R R L L L R R R   L R L R L R L R L R L R

R R R L L L R R R L L L R R R L L L   R L R L R L R L R L R L R L
L L L R R R L L L R R R L L L R R R   L R L R L R L R L R L R L R

R R R L L L L R R R L L L L R R R L L L L R R R L
L L L R R R R L L L R R R R L L L R R R R L L L R

BUZZ ROLL

No drummer's rudimental arsenal would be complete without the buzz roll. The buzz roll is also commonly referred to as the closed roll, since there's no space between the notes, or as the press roll, since it's played by pressing the sticks into the drumhead.

Unlike the rest of the top twelve rudiments, the buzz roll's hand motion is not used in any other rudiment. Nonetheless, the buzz roll is a "can't live without it" rudiment, so it's included here. While it's very easy to play initially, it's difficult to play well so that the buzzes sound consistent and even (like radio static). The buzz roll is an important rudiment to know because buzz strokes are extremely useful for making dynamic music on the drumset.

There are two keys to playing a good-sounding buzz roll. First you need to press the stick into the drum with the ideal amount of pressure (with both hands matching perfectly) and then you need to alternate the hands evenly at a consistent rate.

Let's start by looking at the technique required to play a buzz roll. A first-finger fulcrum should be used with no gap between the thumb and the hand. The thumb should be a bit on the topside of the stick so it can help add pressure down into the drum. (If your thumb is on the side of the stick, then you'll need to add tension elsewhere in the hand in order to compensate for what would otherwise be generated by the thumb.) Press the stick into the drum hard enough to create a buzz sound where no individual strokes can be heard.

At slower speeds, it's helpful to press as hard as necessary to assure a closed buzz sound and then immediately lighten up the pressure in order to get a bit more sustain out of the buzz. Apply as much or as little pressure, using as many or as few fingers as the volume level/stick height, tempo, and drumhead tension dictate, in order to achieve the most seamless sound possible. Most often, you'll be using the first two or three fingers.

When playing very quiet buzz rolls, it's common to only use the end of the first finger (under the fulcrum) since so little pressure is needed to push the stick into the head. As the buzz roll gets louder and the stick heights increase, or as the primary stroke rate gets faster, more fingers can be added since more pressure into the drumhead will be required. More often than not, buzz rolls are played with a pumping forearm motion. The forearms help to relieve the wrists as the tempos get faster.

Although a well-executed buzz roll has no audible rhythm, the primary strokes behind each buzz stroke should be played as a set rhythm. Choosing the best rhythm to use for the primary strokes is important because they set you up to release the buzz roll perfectly in time.

If the primary strokes are played at a rate that's too slow, then each hand's stroke is heard as individual buzz strokes. If the rate is too fast, then it becomes physically stressful to execute the buzz roll. I generally use a 16th-note primary stroke rate for tempos between 100 and 140 bpm. I use a triplet-based based primary stroke rate for tempos between 140 and 180 bpm. For slower tempos, sextuplets can work. And for faster tempos, I'll often go with a rate of 8th notes. Sometimes fivelets (a five-note subdivision) can be perfect for those tempos that fall in the cracks.

The bottom line is that buzz rolls need to be experimented with in order to find the best primary stroke rate and the right amount of pressure into the drum to achieve an even, static sound at each dynamic level and speed.

Do your best to develop the finesse necessary to play a smooth and even-sounding buzz roll, with the primary strokes perfectly in time at various tempos and at various dynamic levels.

PARADIDDLE

```
>                           >
R   L   R   R       L   R   L   L
L   R   L   L       R   L   R   R
```

The paradiddle is one of the most frequently used rudiments, yet many players haven't tapped into its natural ability to develop accent and tap control. If you play paradiddles without a clear accent on the first beat, the rudiment can sound monotonous. But building your paradiddle chops using clear accents—made possible through downstroke/upstroke control—will allow you to play paradiddles and other compound stickings with more dynamic expression.

To begin, let's look at the downstroke and upstroke techniques that are needed to play accented paradiddles. The downstroke starts high (roughly 90 degrees) but stops low after the stroke (around 1" from the head). The upstroke starts low and is lifted back to the "up" position after striking the drum. The key to proper downstrokes is to hit the drum in the same way you would with a free stroke—but immediately after the stick strikes the head, squeeze the stick into the palm in order to stop the stick pointing down with the stick tip close to the drum.

Assuming you've developed the finger control necessary to play diddles (alley-oop or drop-catch at low stick heigh), the biggest challenge with executing paradiddles is having to play a downstroke followed by a light diddle at a lower stick height. Playing on top of the sticks at a slightly higher angle relative to the drum will slightly reduce the accent's rebound, which offers more leverage to stop the stick. (Remember that downstrokes point down.) Also, having the thumb on the topside of the stick, with no gap between the thumb and first finger, will make it much easier to squelch the stick's rebound. Other than the downstroke accent, every other note in a paradiddle should be played with a loose grip where the sticks resonate freely and feel heavy in the hands.

At fast tempos, you'll want to employ the Moeller whip downstroke technique, which is is a modified downstroke where the stroke is played from the forearm with a whipping motion rather than from the wrist. (The wrist stays completely relaxed.) The Moeller whip downstroke is great for playing any rudiment that contains an accent and tap at faster tempos, since it alleviates the wrist's need to perform upstrokes. You'll want to let some of the accent's energy flow into the following diddle. Closing the fingers around the stick a little bit (without hitting the palm of the hand) will help get the stick back down to the drum so that they can play the diddle. At very fast tempos, the paradiddle will be played almost exclusively with forearms and fingers.

Here are technical guidelines for playing paradiddles at various tempos:

Slow: Stop the stick after the accent by squeezing the back of the stick against the palm. Use mainly wrist strokes for all notes.

Medium: Restrict the accent's rebound with the fingers, but allow some of the stick's energy to propel the unaccented notes. Use a combination of wrist and fingers for the inner beats (drop-catch).

Fast: Play accents using a slight Moeller whip stroke. Don't restrict the rebound after accents. Play unaccented inner beats with the fingers. (At very fast tempos, paradiddles must be executed almost exclusively with the forearms and fingers.)

In addition to playing the exercises in this article, be sure to practice paradiddles going evenly from slow to fast to slow over one minute. Gradually adjust your technique as the tempo goes up and down.

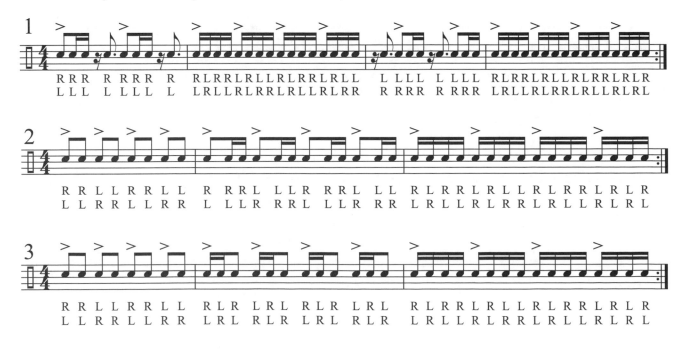

> > > > > > > > > >
R LLRR L   R LLRR L   or   R LL RR L   R LL RR L
L RRLL R   L RRLL R   L RR LL R   L RR LL R

SIX-STROKE ROLL

The six-stroke roll is on our list of the twelve key rudiments because it contains unique hand motions that will open doors to many other rudiments. One of the most important benefits of studying the rudiments is developing individual hand motions that can be applied to other areas of drumming beyond a rudimental context. While that concept is true of the six-stroke roll, this particular rudiment is also incredibly useful when voiced around the drumset. Here we'll look at the techniques you'll need to play six-stroke rolls with strict 16th-note interpretation, as well as the slurred variation that morphs into a sextuplet.

The accents in six-stroke rolls are what gives them flavor (be sure to use downstrokes for these). Here's the key to executing relaxed downstrokes: Begin the motion exactly like a free stroke, but just after the stick hits the head, partially stifle the stick's natural rebound by squeezing the back of the stick with the fingers.

As you learn the six-stroke roll, I recommend making the downstrokes stop at an angle pointing down toward the drum, in order to maximize the dynamic and stick-height differential between the accents and double strokes. Once you master the motion, you can vary the degree of strictness of the downstrokes for different musical applications. Keep in mind that it's important to avoid hitting the accents too hard or with tight strokes that drive through the drumhead. Stay relaxed!

The diddles inside the six-stroke roll should be played low to the drum with a relaxed alley-oop technique. This is where the first stroke is played mainly from the wrist and the second stroke mainly from the fingers. It will look like the hand drops toward the drum on the first stroke of the double, and then your fingers snap out the second stroke by bringing the back of the stick to the palm of the hand. The hand should then lift up for the following accent. If your finger control still needs developing, remember that it's better to play the diddles a bit weakly and bouncy than to stroke them out entirely with the wrists.

The technique used to play six-stroke rolls slowly is different from the one used to play them fast. The downstroke/ upstroke technique for the accents and the alley-oop technique for the diddles won't change, but you'll need to pump your forearms when playing at faster rates. This motion will relieve the building tension in the wrists. When you play six-stroke rolls quickly, it will almost feel like you're playing a continuous double-stroke roll with occasional non-diddled accents. Once you've mastered the six-stroke roll, your hands will be able to hit any accent patterns within a roll.

Practice the following exercises with a metronome (or along to your favorite songs). Don't go any faster than you can play comfortably. You should also practice this rudiment using a slow-fast-slow breakdown evenly over one minute, gradually adjusting your technique as the speed changes.

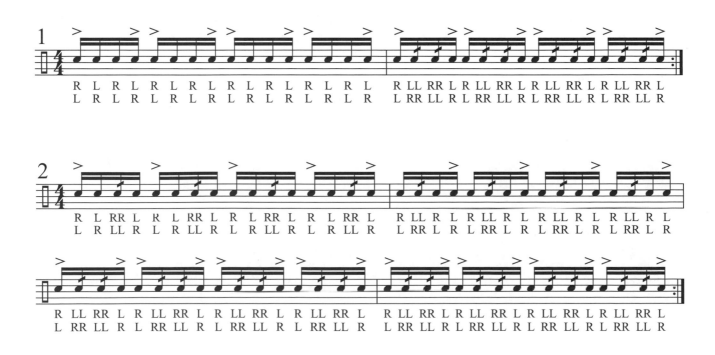

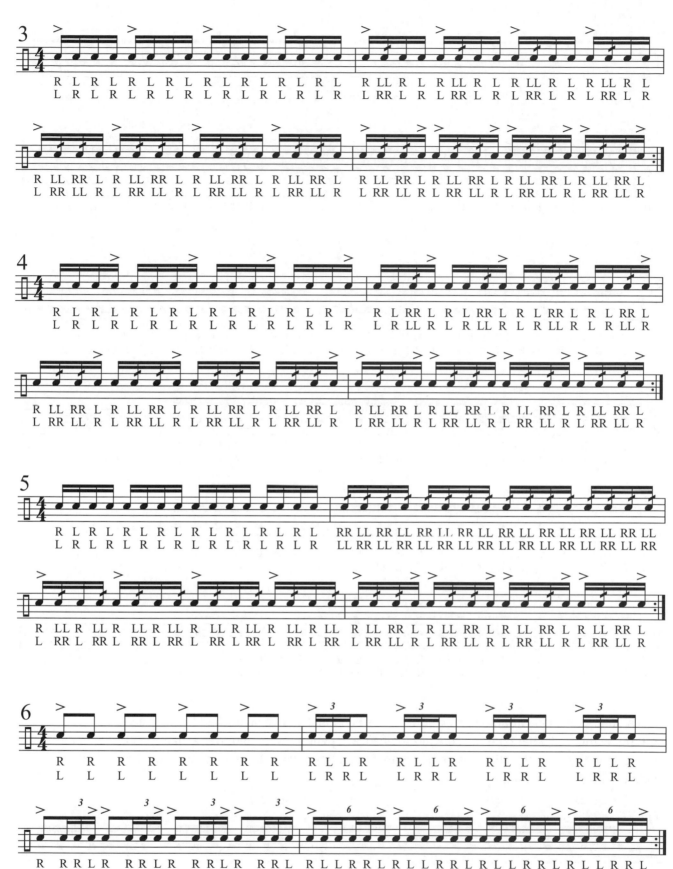

As a bonus, let's look at how the six-stroke roll's hand motion can be applied to other accent patterns within rolls. Here are the son and rumba clave patterns accented over a steady roll. (Note that in this case the stickings do not change with the repeats. Be sure to also play them leading with the left hand.)

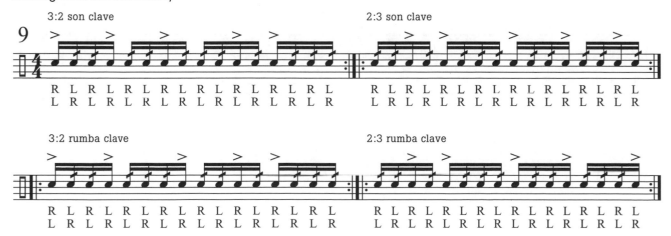

HAND-TO-HAND FLAMS

Playing alternating flams demands a certain amount of chops. Playing fast hand-to-hand flams require a different kind of chops—whipping Moeller strokes. If you can master the technique needed to play hand-to-hand flams at all tempos, your accent/tap motion will become much stronger and faster while requiring less energy.

A flam is simply a grace note tied to a main stroke. The primary note has metric value and should land exactly in time. The grace note is used to add texture and thickness to the sound and should be placed just before the primary note. If the grace note hits at the same time as the primary note, then you're playing a "flat flam," which is actually a double stop (two notes in unison) and not a flam at all.

A player with good control can play both tight flams, where the grace note is placed very close to the primary note, and wide (or fat) flams, where there's a bigger space between the grace note and the primary stroke. Ultimately, grace note placement is a musical choice based on style, drumhead response, and speed.

Let's look at the technique you'll need to play alternating flams at slow and medium speeds. Each hand plays a high accent stroke followed by a low grace note. Use the downstroke/upstroke technique for these. Be sure to squeeze the stick a bit with your fingers after the accent in order to freeze the stick pointing down toward the drum. Then play a relaxed low grace note as an upstroke, since you'll need to lift the stick for the following accent. Avoid hitting the accents extra hard and with tight strokes, where your fingers are squeezing the stick while you play the grace notes. Other than the split second after the accent, when you stifle the stick's rebound, everything should flow smoothly. Note that the downstroke is also commonly referred to as a staccato stroke. *Staccato* is the musical term meaning short and separated, which in this case refers to the accent's hand motion being short and separate from the following grace note's hand motion.

If you tried playing fast hand-to-hand flams using the aforementioned technique, your wrists would tighten up and seize, since there's not enough time to stop the stroke, restart the motion, and then lift up. This is where the Moeller whip stroke comes in to replace the wrist motion with a forearm motion. When you use the forearm, the wrist can relax. Don't stop the stick after the accent. Let the accent stroke's energy flow into the next grace note using the Moeller whip-and-flop technique. This grace note should be played with what I call a Moeller upstroke, where the stick hits the drum as you lift the forearm, with the wrist hanging limp.

The technique behind playing fast hand-to-hand flams with the Moeller technique will be easier to understand as you play Example 1, which isolates the motions in each hand. You should feel like you're playing quarter notes with your forearm while a little rebound stroke drops in on the upbeats. This is the key hand motion for fast hand-to-hand flams. (It's similar to the shoulder/tip hi-hat motion that many drummers use when playing 8th-note grooves.)

Practice the following exercises slowly using the downstroke/upstroke technique—stopping the sticks after the accents—as well as the whipping Moeller technique. (A great way to achieve speed with all rudiments is to practice a fast tempo's technique slowly. I've seen many players struggle to achieve high speeds because they practice only the slower tempo's technique.) Be sure to practice the following exercises using the correct stickings; the stickings marked "T" should be played with both hands in unison. Use a metro-nome or play along with your favorite tunes, and don't go any faster than you can play comfortably. In addition to the exercises provided, practice hand-to-hand flams using the traditional slow-fast-slow breakdown evenly over one minute, gradually changing your technique in correlation with the speed.

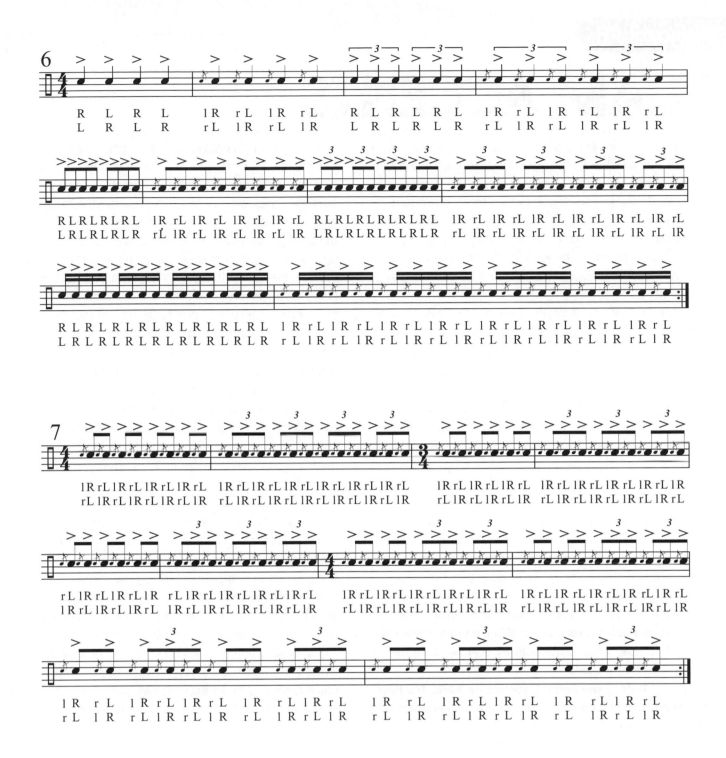

FLAM ACCENTS

The flam accent is included because of its unique hand motion, which involves a downstroke with a quick transition into a low triple beat. Mastering the flam accent will open doors that allow you to play many other rudiments, as well as numerous patterns on the drumset that may seem unrelated. I can't remember the last time I played flam accents on the kit, but because I can do so, my hands have the ability to execute many other useful musical ideas.

To play quality flam accents, we must first take a look at the individual hand motion shown in Exercise 1. Each hand plays a high accent stroke followed by three low tap strokes. Those tap strokes technically consist of an inner beat, a grace note, and another inner beat, but in the flam accent context they're straightened out into one rhythmically even triple beat. (A flam between the two hands is created by laying the accent back just behind the grace note.) The accent will need to be played as a downstroke. Be sure to quickly stifle the stick's rebound after the accent in order to freeze the stick pointing down toward the drum. All activity must stop at this point, so that you can get a fresh start with loose fingers playing the low and relaxed triple beat.

Here are two downstroke tips to help you sidestep common roadblocks:

1. Avoid hitting the accent extra hard with a tight stroke where the fingers are still busy squeezing the stick when they should actually be starting to play the relaxed triple beat.

2. Avoid letting the accent bounce up high, leaving you unable to initiate the triple beat at the correct low stick height. A high bounce can also cause you to play rhythmically late as you wait for the stick to get back down to the drumhead.

Playing flam accents at different speeds will require little changes in technique. At slower tempos, you can play all of the strokes easily using the wrists. As you get to a medium speed, you'll need to start using the "alley-oop-oop" finger-control technique on the triple beat to support the second and third beats. Otherwise the wrist will get tight as it struggles to keep up, or the beats will weakly bounce down to nothing. As you get faster, you will eventually hit a speed where there isn't enough time to completely stop the stick between the accent and the low triple beat. At this point it's okay to let a bit of the accent's energy flow into the low triple beat instead of completely stopping the stick. The fingers should now squelch some of the accent's rebound as they push the stick back to the head to start the triple beat. The faster you can go while still stopping the stick for controlled stick heights and dynamic contrast, the better. After all, if the triple beats bounce up too high, then you no longer have an accent.

Practice the following exercises slowly, and gradually work your way up in tempo. (In the stickings, lowercase letters represent soft grace notes.) Keep in mind that the best way to achieve speed with all rudiments is to practice many correct repetitions using the various techniques that are required for different tempos. In addition to the exercises provided, be sure to practice this rudiment with the traditional slow-fast-slow breakdown evenly over one minute, gradually changing your technique in correlation with the speed. If you practice this rudimental breakdown and these exercises for even five to ten minutes a day, you'll be amazed at how much your hands improve.

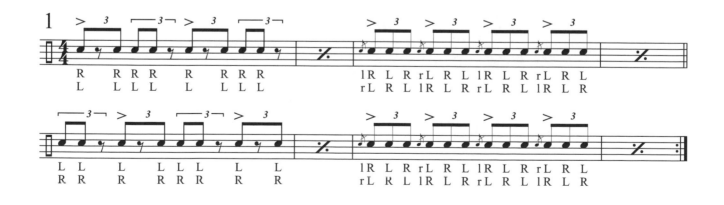

2

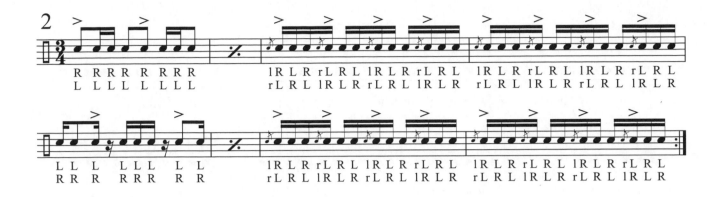

R R R R R R R R
L L L L L L L L

lRLR rLRL lRLR rLRL   lRLR rLRL lRLR rLRL
rLRL lRLR rLRL lRLR   rLRL lRLR rLRL lRLR

L L L L L L L L
R R R R R R R R

lRLR rLRL lRLR rLRL   lRLR rLRL lRLR rLRL
rLRL lRLR rLRL lRLR   rLRL lRLR rLRL lRLR

For variations on the exercises below, try playing only the bars that start with the right
hand, and then only the bars that start with the left hand. The goal is to keep the leading
hand consistent while coordinating the opposite hand's parts.

3

R RRR R RRR   R RRR R RRR   L LLL L LLL   L LLL L LLL

lR RRR lR RRR   lR RRR lR RRR   rL LLL rL LLL   rL LLL rL LLL

lR R rLR lR R rLR   lR R rLR lR R rLR   rL L lRL rL L lRL   rL L lRL rL L lRL

lRLRrLRLlRLRrLRL   lRLRrLRLlRLRrLR   rLRLlRLRrLRLlRLR   rLRLlRLRrLRLlRL

4

R RRR R RRR   R RRR R RRR   L LLL L LLL   L LLL L LLL

lR R R R lR R R R   lR R R R lR R R R   rL L L L L rL L L L L   rL L L L L rL L L L

lR R rLR lR R rLR   lR R rLR lR R rLR   rL L lRL rL L lRL   rL L lRL rL L lRL

lRLR rLRL lRLR rLRL   lRLR rLRL lRLR rLR   rLRL lRLR rLRL lRLR   rLRL lRLR rLRL lRL

43

5

R R R R R RRR   R RRR R RRR   L LLL L LLL   L LLL L LLL

RLRRR RLRRR   RLRRR RLRRR   LRLLL LRLLL   LRLLL LRLLL

RLRRRLRLRRRL RLRRRLRLRRR   LRLLLRLRLLLR LRLLLRLRLLL

lRLRRRL lRLRRRL   lRLRRRL lRLRRR   rLRLLLR rLRLLLR   rLRLLLR rLRLLL

lRLR rLRL lRLR rLRL   lRLR rLRL lRLR rLR   rLRL lRLR rLRL lRLR   rLRL lRLR rLRL lRL

6

R R R R R RRR   R RRR R RRR   L LLL L LLL   L LLL L LLL

RLRRR RLRRR   RLRRR RLRRR   LRLLL LRLLL   LRLLL LRLLL

RLRRRLRLRRRL RLRRRLRLRRR   LRLLLRLRLLLR LRLLLRLRLLL

lRLRRRL lRLRRRL   lRLRRRL lRLRRR   rLRLLLR rLRLLLR   rLRLLLR rLRLLL

lRLR rLRL lRLR rLRL   lRLR rLRL lRLR rLR   rLRL lRLR rLRL lRLR   rLRL lRLR rLRL lRL

```
>           >           >           >
L R    R  R L   L    L R    R  R L   L
R L    L  L R   R    R L    L  L R   R
```

FLAM TAP

The flam tap is on our list because it requires a unique hand motion where strokes decrescendo after an initial accent, without the stick stopping. Each hand plays an accent, tap, and grace note, in that order.

When going from an accent to a tap, we would usually play a downstroke in order to achieve the proper stick height and dynamic contrast. With the flam tap, however, at even a medium tempo there isn't enough time to stop and then restart the stick's motion at a lower height after the accent. With this in mind, we need to make each hand play rebounding strokes that decrescendo while maintaining the stick's energy from the initial accent (no-chop flop-and-drop). The flam tap will train your hands to use this vital hand motion, which has built-in dynamics, flows well, and will be very useful for making music around the kit.

To play flam taps with maximum quality, let's first take a look at the individual hand motion shown in Example 1. As written, each hand plays a high accent stroke followed by a low tap stroke and a grace note. (In the stickings, lowercase letters represent grace notes.) Usually the grace note is pushed ahead rhythmically, in order for it to precede the following hand's accent. But in flam taps the strokes are straightened out into an even triple beat so that they flow smoothly. (The flams are created by placing the accents just *behind* the grace notes.) The technique used for the accent and the following tap falls somewhere between a full stroke and a downstroke, since the stick naturally drops down to a lower stick height and dynamic level while maintaining some rebound. The grace note will simply be an upstroke, in order to set the hand upward for the next accented triple beat.

Playing flam taps should feel like you're playing weak triple beats or simply letting the sticks bounce three times on the drumhead. Those with well-developed "alley-oop-oop" finger control for playing strong triple beats (where all three beats are at roughly the same stick height and dynamic level) should pay particular attention, since strong inner beats will diminish the impact of the accents. The more you can exaggerate the contrast in stick height and dynamics, the better, since you're emulating an accented flam and an unaccented tap. Much finesse will be necessary to play bouncy threes and flam taps with rhythmic accuracy. Here are quick tips for playing flam taps:

1. Avoid hitting the accents extra hard with tight strokes, where the fingers are squeezing the stick when they should be playing the second and third beats of the triple beat.

2. Avoid letting the accents bounce up high, leaving you unable to differentiate dynamically between the accent and the tap.

3. Be sure to play the first stroke with a big accent from a high stick level. Don't cheat the accent in the interest of playing the subsequent beats low.

To play flam taps at different speeds, you'll need to modify your technique. At slower speeds, all of the strokes can be played easily using the wrists, with downstrokes on the accents for clear stick height and dynamic contrast. As you get to medium speeds and higher, you'll need to start letting the stick bounce loosely from the accent to the second and third beats as explained above; otherwise the wrists will tighten up as they struggle to keep up with the tempo. When you practice this rudiment from slow to fast to slow over one minute, the change in technique should happen gradually as the tempo increases or decreases.

Practice the following exercises slowly, and gradually work your way up in tempo. Keep in mind that the best way to achieve speed with all rudiments is to practice many correct repetitions using the next faster tempo's technique. In addition to the exercises provided, be sure to practice this rudiment with the traditional slow-fast-slow breakdown evenly over one minute, gradually changing the technique in correlation with the speed.

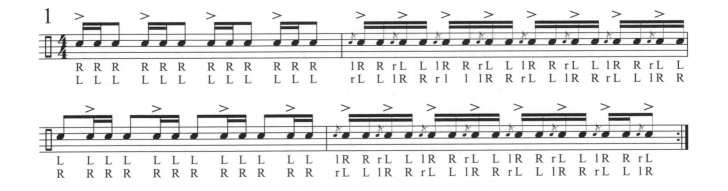

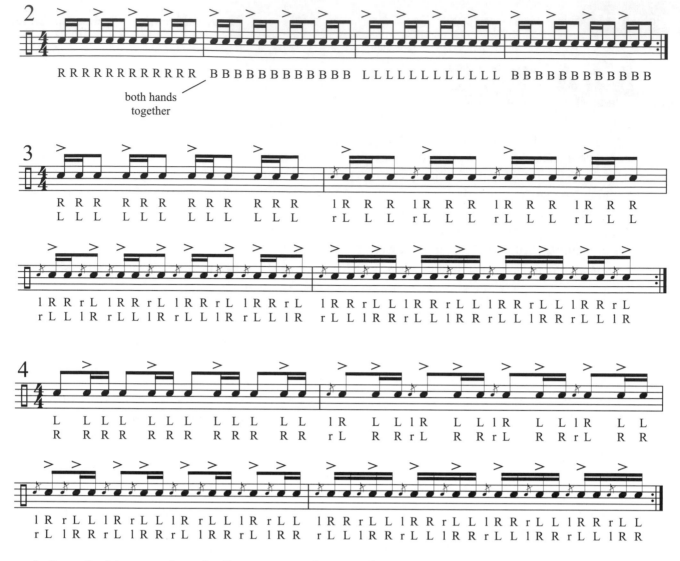

2

R R R R R R R R R R R   B B B B B B B B B B B B   L L L L L L L L L L L L   B B B B B B B B B B B B

both hands together

3

R R R R R R R R R R R R   lR R R lR R R lR R R lR R R
L L L L L L L L L L L L   rL L L rL L L rL L L rL L L

lRRrL lRRrL lRRrL lRRrL   lRRrLL lRRrLL lRRrLL lRRrL
rLLlR rLLlR rLLlR rLLlR   rLLlRR rLLlRR rLLlRR rLLlR

4

L L L L L L L L L L L L   lR L L lR L L lR L L lR L L
R R R R R R R R R R R R   rL R R rL R R rL R R rL R R

lR rLL lR rLL lR rLL lR rLL   lRRrLL lRRrLL lRRrLL lRRrLL
rL lRR rL lRR rL lRR lR RR   rLL lRRrLL lRRrLL lRRrLL lRR

In these final two exercises, the flam taps are taken out of their usual alternating context. When you place them in different rhythmic locations, they actually become Swiss Army triplets and single-flammed mills.

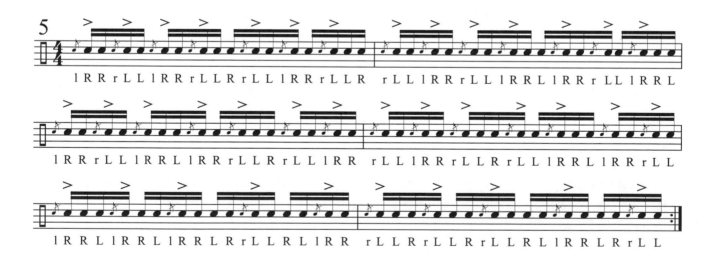

5

lRRrLL lRRrLLRrLL lRRrLL   rLL lRRrLL lRRL lRRrLL lRRL

lRRrLL lRRL lRRrLLRrLL lRR   rLL lRRrLLRrLL lRRL lRRrLL

lRRL lRRL lRRLRrLL RL lRR   rLLRrLLRrLLRL lRRRLrLL

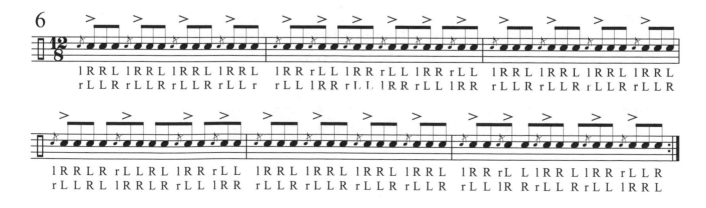

6

lRRL lRRL lRRL lRRL   lRRrLL lRRrLL lRRrLL   lRRL lRRL lRRL lRRL
rLLR rLLR rLLR rLLr   rLL lRR rLL lRR rLL lRR   rLLR rLLR rLLR rLLR

lRRLR rLLRL lRRrLL   lRRL lRRL lRRL   lRRrLL lRRL lRRL lRRrLLR
rLLRL lRRRLr LLlRR   rLLRr LLRrLLR rLLr   LLlR RrLLRrLLlRRL

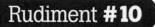

INVERTED FLAM TAP

Some may assume that the inverted flam tap is similar to the standard flam tap, which we covered in the previous chapter, but the inverted flam tap actually sounds quite different—and playing it requires a totally different technique.

The inverted flam tap looks like the standard flam tap until you notice the unique sticking. Unlike the standard flam tap where the tap follows an accent with the same hand, the tap now *precedes* the accent with the same hand. This is what makes the rudiment tricky. The challenge is to quickly get to the accent after the tap without a rhythmic delay or tension as you lift up the stick. Using the Moeller whip stroke makes it much easier to achieve the proper stick height for the accent. The goal in learning this rudiment is to have well-trained hands that can effortlessly play patterns such as shuffle grooves, where taps immediately precede accents.

To review, a Moeller whip downstroke is a modified downstroke that's played from the forearm with a whipping motion rather than from the wrist. As a general rule, the Moeller whip stroke should be implemented when you need to quickly get the stick up for accents at speeds where the wrist would otherwise struggle to do so. Simply put, the Moeller stroke allows you to smoothly play accent patterns from your forearm with a relaxed hand, instead of overworking your wrist.

Let's first look at the technique necessary to play inverted flam taps at a slow speed. Each hand plays two low taps (the first of which is a grace note) followed by a high accent stroke. At this tempo you can easily play a low tap stroke, an upstroke, and a downstroke using the wrists. If you try to play inverted flam taps at a medium or fast speed with the

same technique, your wrists will tighten up, since there's not enough time for the hands to play an upstroke preceding the accented flam. Again, this is where the Moeller stroke comes in and replaces the wrist motion with a forearm motion.

The tap immediately preceding the accented flam will be played with a Moeller upstroke, where the stick just happens to hit the drum as you pick up the forearm and let the wrist hang limp. Regardless of the tempo, be sure to quickly stifle the stick's rebound after the accent in order to freeze the stick pointing down toward the drum (Moeller whip downstroke). This will help you maintain a good stick-height differential between the accents and taps in order to achieve maximum musical contrast. Also be sure to coordinate the two hands so that the flams are consistent from hand to hand; if one hand's flam is wider than the other's, then that hand needs to better develop the quick Moeller whip stroke.

Practice the following exercises slowly and work your way up, most often using the faster tempo's technique, which incorporates the Moeller whip stroke. The best way to achieve speed with all rudiments is to practice the fast tempo's technique slowly. I've seen many players fail to achieve high speeds because they practice only the slower tempo's speed-limiting technique. Be sure to practice the following exercises with the correct stickings (lowercase letters represent grace notes). Use a metronome or play along with your favorite tunes, and don't go any faster than you can play comfortably. Also practice this rudiment using the traditional slow-fast-slow breakdown evenly over one minute, gradually changing the technique in correlation with the speed.

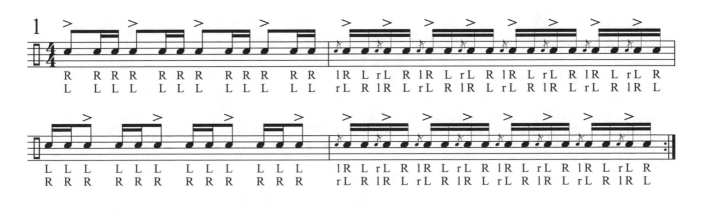

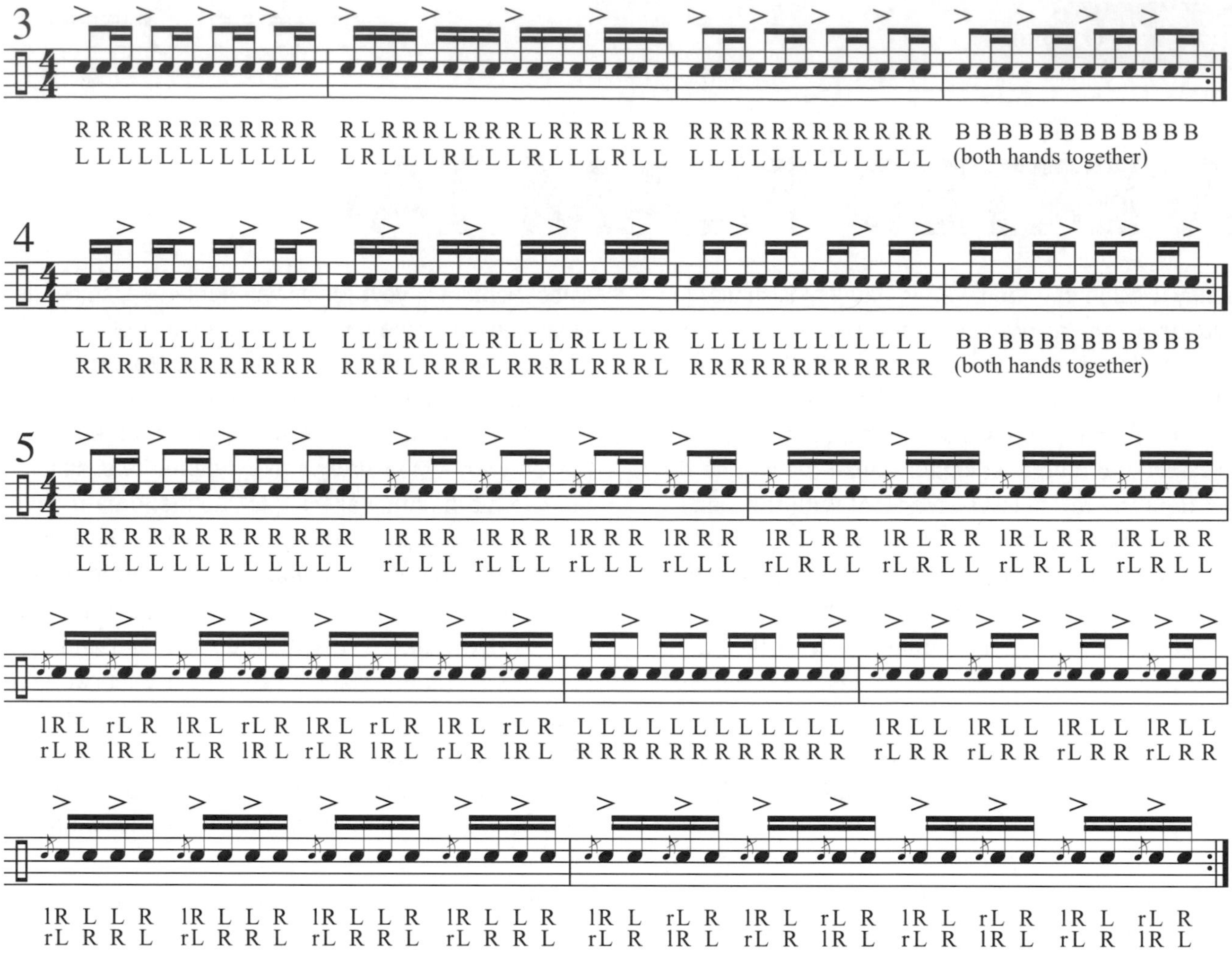

3

RRRRRRRRRRRR RLRRRLRRRLRRRLRR RRRRRRRRRRRR BBBBBBBBBBBB
LLLLLLLLLLLL LRLLLRLLLRLLLRLL LLLLLLLLLLLL (both hands together)

4

LLLLLLLLLLLL LLLRLLLRLLLRLLLR LLLLLLLLLLLL BBBBBBBBBBBB
RRRRRRRRRRRR RRRLRRRLRRRLRRRL RRRRRRRRRRRR (both hands together)

5

RRRRRRRRRRRR lRRR lRRR lRRR lRRR lRLRR lRLRR lRLRR lRLRR
LLLLLLLLLLLL rLLL rLLL rLLL rLLL rLRLL rLRLL rLRLL rLRLL

lRL rLR lRL rLR lRL rLR lRL rLR LLLLLLLLLLLL lRLL lRLL lRLL lRLL
rLR lRL rLR lRL rLR lRL rLR lRL RRRRRRRRRRRR rLRR rLRR rLRR rLRR

lRLLR lRLLR lRLLR lRLLR lRL rLR lRL rLR lRL rLR lRL rLR
rLRRL rLRRL rLRRL rLRRL rLR lRL rLR lRL rLR lRL rLR lRL

For variations on exercises 6 and 7, try playing only the bars that start with the right hand and then only the bars that start with the left hand. The goal is to keep the leading hand consistent while coordinating the opposite hand's parts.

6

RLLRLLRLLRLL LRRLRRLRRLRR lRLL lRLL lRLL lRLL rLRR rLRR rLRR rLRR

lR L rL L lR L rL L lR L rL L lR L rL L rL R lR R rL R lR R rL R lR R rL R lR R

lRL rLR lRL rLR lRL rLR lRL rLR lRL rLR lRL rLR lRL rLR lRL rLR lRL rLR lRL rLR lRL rLR

7

R LRR LRR LRR LR L RLL RLL RLL RL lR LR lR LR lR LR lR LR LR

rLRL rLRL rLRL rLRL lR rLR lR rLR lR rLR lR rLR rL lRL rL lRL rL lRL rL lRL

lRL rLR lRL rLR lRL rLR lRL rLR lRL rLR lRL rLR lRL rLR lRL rLR lRL rLR lRL rLR lRL rLR

DRAG

LLR   RRL
RRL   LLR

Drags are grace notes with no true metric value of their own; they must be tied to their primary notes. They're often interpreted as closed buzz strokes, but for our purposes we should play them exactly as written, as open double-stroke diddles. (Once you've mastered open drags, it's a good idea to go back and practice them as buzzes for variation.) Drags are also open to interpretation. They can be played wide, with a lot of space between the notes, or tight, where the notes are very close together and played as close to the primary note as possible without overlapping. (The style of music you're playing, as well as the tension of your drumhead, will be determining factors in how you phrase drags.) At faster tempos, it's practical and very common for drags to be played as precise rhythms, since there isn't enough time to play them tighter.

It's very simple to play drags slowly; just play a low diddle before a downstroke accent. The downstroke is stopped with the bead of the stick low to the drumhead, which ensures that you're ready to initiate the next low diddle with the same hand. At this slow tempo, the drag is simply played as a low diddle using the wrist/finger alley-oop technique.

At fast tempos, the technique for playing drags changes drastically, and we need to implement a new hand motion. This is where the true value of the rudiment shows up. In this situation, there's no time to stop the stick with a downstroke preceding the drag, since doing so would result in slowing down the tempo and tightening up the hands. (You're asking too much of your hands to execute all

of these motions in such a short amount of time.) To avoid this tension, the accent should rebound smoothly into the drag so that some of the accent's energy flows through. The fingers must then squeeze out a low diddle with no prep time, and that's the key hand motion—it's all about finger control. It's important to note that at this fast, flowing speed, stick heights will not be as defined as they were at a slower tempo, where there was time to stop the stick low to the drum.

It's extremely helpful to grip the stick between the thumb and first finger (the "first-finger fulcrum") for rudiments like this that require finger finesse. Having the fulcrum in the front of the hand, with the thumb on the topside of the stick and no gap between the thumb and first finger, gives the end of the first finger and middle finger good access to the stick for small, quick motions. At tempos requiring this level of finger finesse, the back fingers have more distance to travel to track with the stick, and will therefore sometimes drop off completely. It's wise to practice using multiple fulcrum points, because the more techniques that are available to you, the more options you have when executing your musical ideas. Switching on the fly from one technique to another will happen automatically once your hands are trained to know which one has the path of least resistance for various drumming tasks.

Be sure to practice this rudiment using the slow-fast-slow breakdown, gradually changing the technique in correlation to the tempo.

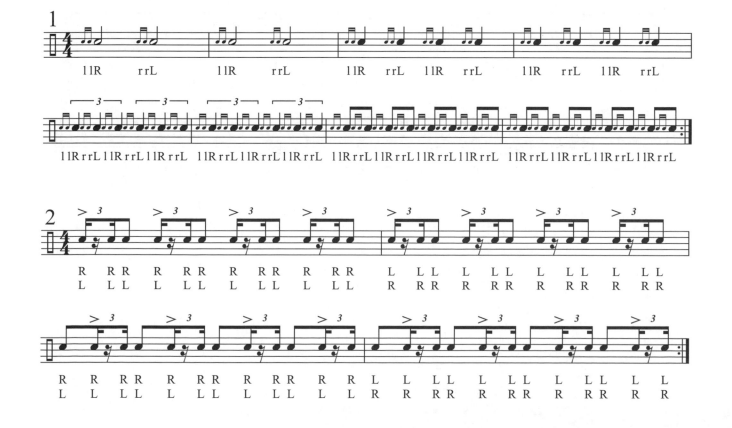

In examples 3–6, notice that the drags at the end of each hand's phrase are written as 16th-note diddles. When played fast, drags will default to this rhythm, rather than being played as grace notes inserted just before the primary note. Work up the tempo on these exercises until they sound like drags and not simple 16th-note rhythms.

DRAGADIDDLE

RR L R R LL R L L   RRL R R LL R L L
LL R L L RR L R R   LLR L L RR R R

The dragadiddle is basically a paradiddle with an accented drag (or diddle) played on the downbeat. The focus within this rudiment is the accented drag (which could be a rudiment all to itself called the "drag accent"). The unique hand motion of the accented drag should be played using the alley-oop wrist/finger free stroke/downstroke combination.

Since the taps following the accented drag need to be played at a low stick height, play the accented drag as a free stroke and a downstroke in very quick succession. In these exercises, we will go beyond the basic rudiment by incorporating accented drags into other vocabulary. The goal is to be able to play a diddle on any accented note in order to have more musical options at your disposal.

The accented drag at the beginning of the dragadiddle is what gives this rudiment its dynamic flavor. You want to differentiate as much as possible between the accented drag and the following low taps. It's wise to think of the accented drag as two separate accented notes in order to avoid crushing the diddle both dynamically and rhythmically. The first beat of the diddle should be played mainly from the wrist as a high free stroke. The second beat should be played mainly from the fingers as an accelerated downstroke, in order to stop the stick low and pointing down toward the drumhead.

Avoid hitting the first accent too hard. It needs to rebound back up so that the fingers have the chance to play the second stroke at an equally strong dynamic level. The second beat of the diddle (the "oop" of the alley-oop) should feel like a slam dunk into the drumhead. You can even think about accenting the second beat of the diddle more than the first.

After the initial accented drag, play the following low tap and double with a loose wrist and fingers so that the stick feels heavy and resonates freely in the hand. The key is to completely separate the low notes from the previous accented drag so that their flow is not affected by the downstroke.

The technique used to play dragadiddles slowly is a bit different from the technique used to play them at medium and fast tempos. As dragadiddles get faster, you'll need to add some forearm to the initial stroke or else the wrists will start to tense up. The low inner beats following the accented drag will require more finger control as the tempo increases. Just make sure that the fingers aren't squeezing the stick against the palm of the hand on the low notes. If your finger control is still a work in progress, remember that it's better to play weak and bouncy diddles than to stroke them out with the wrists. Once the dragadiddle is mastered, your hands will be trained with the motions necessary to play an accented drag at any volume within any meter.

The following exercises build the basic dragadiddle and then apply the drag accent to various other paradiddle rudiments. We'll also work on playing accented drags in a grid format and within some traditional clave patterns. Be sure to practice these exercises with the correct stickings. Use a metronome (or play along with your favorite tunes), and don't go any faster than you can play comfortably. In addition to the exercises provided, be sure to practice this rudiment with the rudimental breakdown. If you practice these exercises for as little as five to ten minutes a day, you'll be amazed at how much your hands improve.

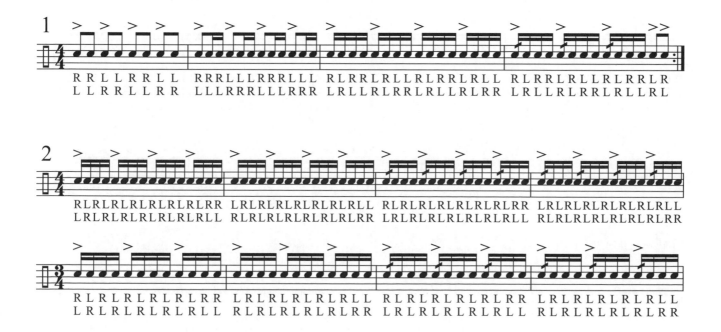

1

R R L L R R L L   R R R L L L R R R L L L   R L R R L R L L R L R R L R L L   R L R R L R L L R L R R L R
L L R R L L R R   L L L R R R L L L R R R   L R L L R L R R L R L L R L R R   L R L L R L R R L R L L R L

2

R L R L R L R L R L R L R R   L R L R L R L R L R L R L L   R L R L R L R L R L R L R R   L R L R L R L R L R L R L L
L R L R L R L R L R L R L L   R L R L R L R L R L R L R R   L R L R L R L R L R L R L L   R L R L R L R L R L R L R R

R L R L R L R L R L R R   L R L R L R L R L R L L   R L R L R L R L R L R R   L R L R L R L R L R L L
L R L R L R L R L R L L   R L R L R L R L R L R R   L R L R L R L R L R L L   R L R L R L R L R L R R

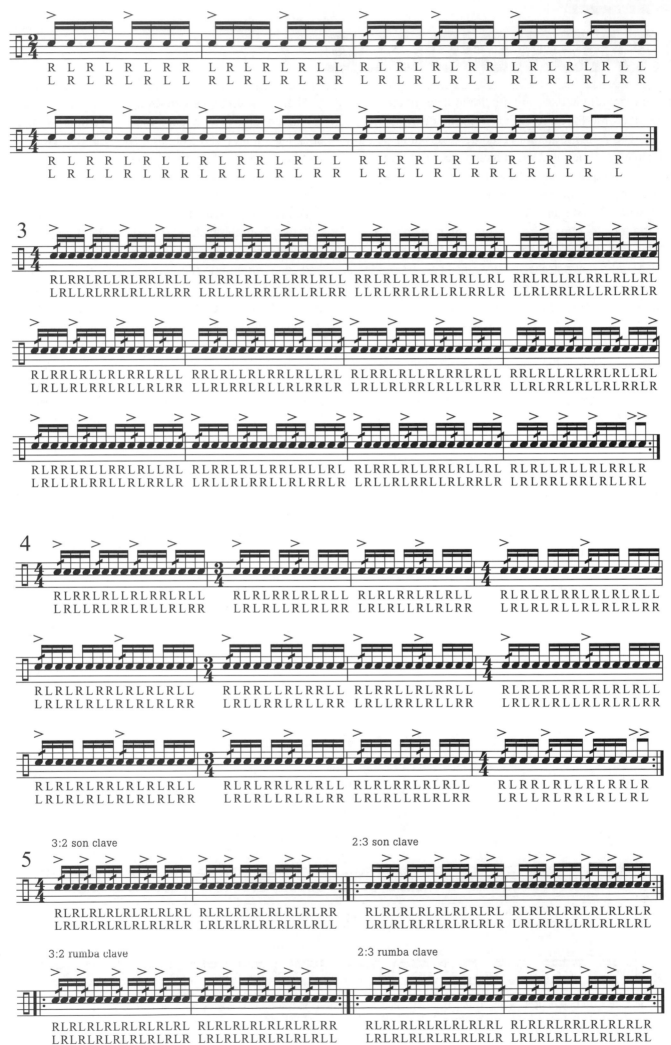

Section 3: CHOPS BUILDERS

INTRODUCTION

Welcome to Chops Builders! In this series of exercises, we're going to be reinforcing and developing specific techniques, hand motions, and coordination, while also sneaking in a bit of useful vocabulary. If you're feeling confident with the top twelve rudiments, then your hands are trained with all of the necessary motions to play these exercises, which develop some additional coordination. You'll find many of the exercises to be great warm-ups when you need to get your hands going in a hurry. Have fun and play great!

Sally Somers

ACCENTS/TAPS

We're starting with accent/tap exercises that consist of groups of twos, threes, and fours played with an accent on the first beat. The lead hand plays the accent and the main grouping, while the other hand plays various "fill-ins."

In each example, the lead hand plays the same continuous pattern. The goal is to coordinate the opposite hand's fill-ins so that the flow of the lead hand never changes.

There are two techniques that you can use to play these exercises: Wrist turns using free strokes, downstrokes, upstrokes, and taps, or the Moeller whip-stroke combination where the accents are played with a whipping motion and the tap strokes flow together. Both techniques are great, and each has its advantages, depending on the situation. Since well-trained hands will naturally take the path of least resistance, a well-rounded player with command of both approaches will find the choice between the two techniques will be automatic. (There are also gradients in between the two methods.) Having great technique allows you to think about music instead of how you're playing the instrument.

Wrist Strokes

First let's look at the approach using freestrokes, downstrokes, taps, and upstrokes. Sets of two notes should be played as a downstroke and an upstroke. Sets of three notes are played as a downstroke, a tap (or a low free stroke), and an upstroke. Sets of four notes are played as a downstroke, two taps, and an upstroke. The stick should stop quickly after each downstroke, with the tip pointing down toward the drum so that the following upstroke or tap can be played with loose hands. This technique is great for slow to medium tempos but does have its limitations at high speeds.

Moeller Strokes

At faster rates, the Moeller whip-stroke combination (whip-and-flop) is great for accent patterns because it allows the wrists to take a break. We'll use whipping Moeller accents, bounce taps, and Moeller upstrokes (where the stick taps the drum as the forearm lifts and the hand drops). Since you'll be going too fast to stop the stick after the accent, all of the notes—including the accent—will flow together so you can conserve energy. The sets of two notes should be played with a Moeller whip stroke and a Moeller upstroke. Sets of three are played as a Moeller whip stroke, a bounce tap, and a Moeller upstroke. Sets of four are played as a Moeller stroke, two bounce taps, and a Moeller upstroke. (As you get into groups of four and higher, finger control will become necessary in order to keep the taps going, since the accent's energy will gradually dissipate.)

With the Moeller whip stroke, the accent is created more through velocity than stick height. Therefore stick heights will not be as strict as they are in the wrist-turn techniques. The Moeller accent strokes should bounce back up somewhat freely, in order to transfer much of the accent's energy into the following tap or taps. Make sure the forearm lifts the stick for the Moeller upstroke only on the last tap preceding the accent. Otherwise the rebound potential of the taps is reduced, the sound of the taps changes, and the velocity of the upcoming Moeller stroke is slowed down preemptively. If you're used to stricter playing techniques, this method will feel a bit lazy and out of control. But here it's all about finesse and doing as little physical work as possible.

Keep the Lead Hand Flowing

In the following exercise, the lead hand's motion remains unchanged throughout, and the motion of the fill-in hand always matches that of the lead hand. The fill-in hand will be added and taken away in different positions relative to the lead hand. The challenge is to coordinate the fill-in hand's entrance to be seamless with the lead hand.

When you add the fill-ins using the Moeller whip-and-flop motion, be sure to initiate the stroke by dragging up the relaxed hand and stick with the forearm. (The hand should droop preceding the whipped accent.) Use a Moeller upstroke—with a drooping prep motion—if the fill-in starts with a tap preceding a whipped accent. This prep gets the fill-in hand started with the correct Moeller whip-and-flop motion, which will continue throughout.

During the double-stop patterns, you want to play with the hands perfectly together. If there's any flamming, you're not playing accurately and your hands are likely not operating the same way technically. It's important to master these double-stops, because if the hands aren't playing in perfect unison, they won't be able to alternate evenly either. Be sure to watch your arms, hands, and sticks, and try to create a mirror image between the hands when playing the double-stops.

When you play these exercises at slower tempos using wrist-turn techniques, try to make it look and sound perfect—just like a machine. When you play them using the Moeller technique, try to make it feel like a constant flow of strokes, with occasional forearm pumps to whip out the accents. Mastering these exercises using both technical approaches at many different speeds will provide you with more ways to make more music.

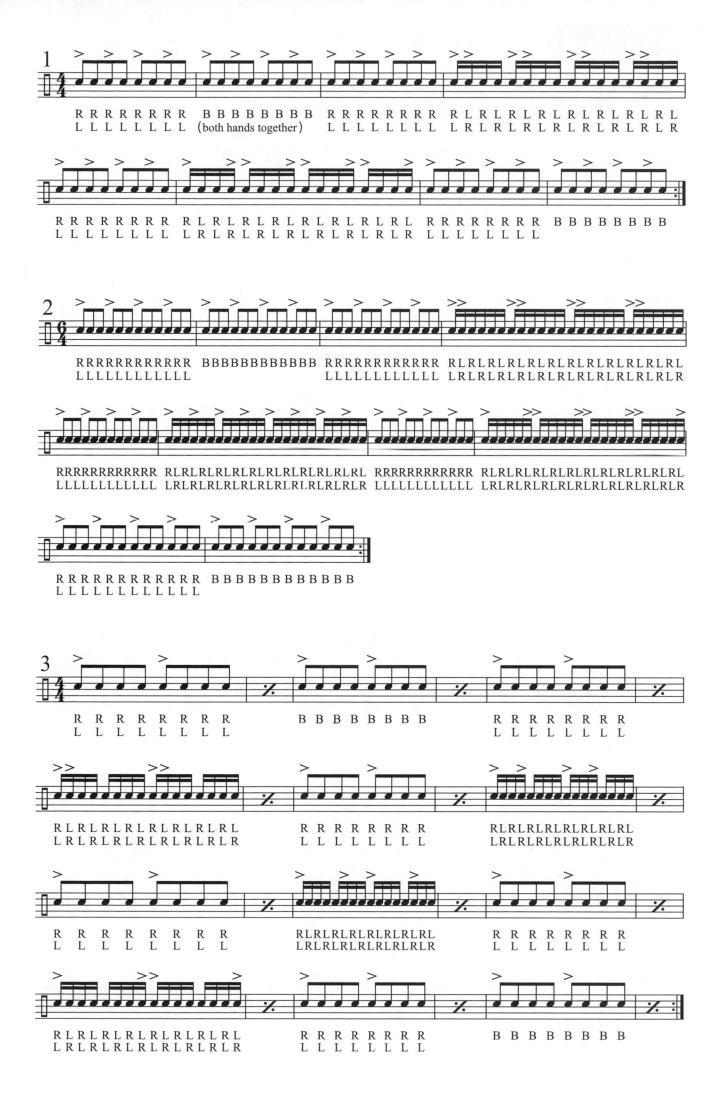

DIDDLES AND ROLLS

These exercises cover most of the combinations of diddles and rolls that you'll encounter, and built into the patterns are the following rudiments: drags, ruffs, five-stroke rolls, six-stroke rolls, and seven-stroke rolls. There's no need to think about these rudiments individually as you work through the examples, though. Just find a comfortable flow and make the exercises groove with relaxed hands. Once you have all of these patterns programmed within your rudimental arsenal, you can use whichever one fits your musical whim behind the kit.

Mastery of the double-stroke roll will help with all of these diddle/roll patterns. Use the alley-oop wrist/finger combination to play open diddles, and avoid weakly bounced or stiffly stroked-out diddles. There are two-count check patterns preceding each diddle or roll pattern, which set up the hand motions that you should use for the diddles and rolls. With the exception of adding

forearm to ease the wrist's workload while playing diddle/roll patterns at fast tempos, the timing, stick heights, stick angles, wrist/finger ratio, velocity, and volume of the strokes should match between the check and the diddle/roll pattern. Focus on a consistent hand motion more than on the individual diddle/roll patterns for the best possible timing and steadiness.

Practice these exercises with a metronome or recorded music so that good timing will become a habit. Avoid playing at a tempo that is too fast to be comfortable. It's important to practice using the correct hand motions and coordination. Feel free to isolate any pattern that is uncomfortable, and be sure to take the repeats, which change the exercises to left-hand lead. Remember that as you get faster you'll need to add the forearms, lower the stick heights, and lighten up your touch.

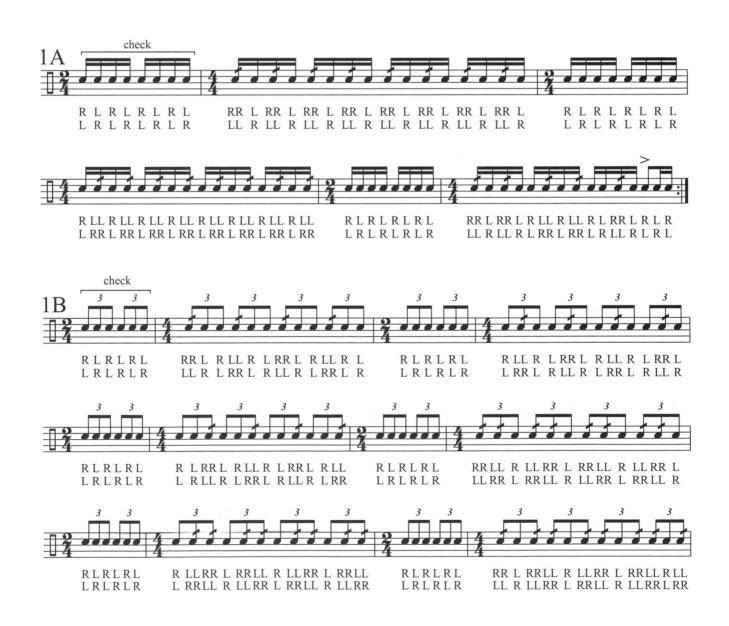

In these exercises we'll add non-diddled accents within rolls.

TRIP STEPPER

In order to warm up different muscle groups as quickly as possible, I find it helpful to change up the physical demands put on the hands. A warm-up exercise I call "trip stepper" accomplishes this by switching from accents and taps, which require downstrokes and upstrokes, to straight accented singles, which should be played as free strokes. The exercise consists of adding accents to and subtracting accents from 16th-note triplets, one 8th note's worth at a time. Trip stepper may look like a long exercise, but once you understand the formula you'll be able to play the entire thing without needing to read it. Your hands should start to feel good after just one time through.

Let's start with a quick review of the necessary techniques. The free stroke (aka legato or full stroke) is a simple rebound stroke, or a dribble of the stick. Using wrist and fingers, throw the stick toward the drum, let it hit the drum loosely with all of its velocity, and then let it rebound back up to the height it started from. Resist any temptation to hold on to the stick tightly or pick the stick up.

The downstroke is a high stroke where the stick stops low to the drum. A downstroke should be played exactly like a free stroke, until just after hitting the head. The stick's natural rebound should then be stifled by squeezing the back of the stick into the palm of the hand. The

stick should be stopped near the drumhead so it's ready for a fresh start on the following relaxed low tap strokes. Keep in mind that there are varying degrees of strictness with downstrokes, but if they come up too much, there won't be enough dynamic contrast between the high accents and low taps. The upstroke used to return the stick to the high accent height is simply a low stroke that's lifted up after hitting the drum.

Now let's look at where and when to apply those techniques in the exercise. The accents that are followed by low taps should be played as downstrokes. All the other free, up, and tap strokes should flow freely and be played as relaxed rebounding strokes. It's especially important to stay loose on all of the low strokes. Listen to the sound of the wood as it resonates within your loose hands on the taps. Every accent that isn't followed by a low tap should also resonate freely as the stick rebounds. Pay close attention to the sound and pitch of your notes—they can really tell a tale about your hand technique, especially when you're playing on a practice pad.

Start slowly to avoid putting stress on your hands, and be sure to play the exercise with the correct stickings. Settle into a nice mental zone, and groove along with good time. Loop through trip stepper as many times as you like. Your hands will soon be feeling great!

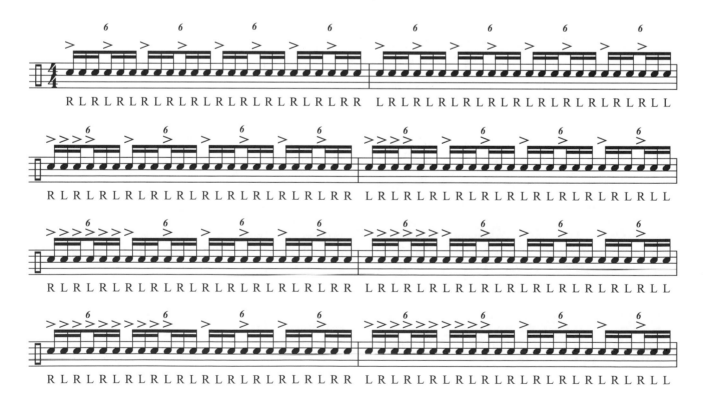

R L R L R L R L R L R L R L R L R L R R   L R L R L R L R L R L R L R L R L R L L

R L R L R L R L R L R L R L R L R L R R   L R L R L R L R L R L R L R L R L R L L

R L R L R L R L R L R L R L R L R L R R   L R L R L R L R L R L R L R L R L R L L

R L R L R L R L R L R L R L R L R L R R   L R L R L R L R L R L R L R L R L R L L

R L R L R L R L R L R L R L R L R L R L   R L R L R L R L R L R L R L R L R L R L

R L R L R L R L R L R L R L R L R L R R   L R L R L R L R L R L R L R L R L R L L

R L R L R L R L R L R L R L R L R L R R   L R L R L R L R L R L R L R L R L R L L

R L R L R L R L R L R L R L R L R L R R   L R L R L R L R L R L R L R L R L R L L

R L R L R L R L R L R L R L R L R L R R   L R L R L R L R L R L R L R L R L R L L

R L R L R L R L R L R L R L R L R L R R   L R L R L R L R L R L R L R L R L R L L

R L R L R L R L R L R L R L R L R L R R   L R L R L R L R L R L R L R L R L R L L

HAIRTA

Now let's look at a modern rudiment known as the hairta. The strange name is onomatopoeia—if you roll the "r" with your tongue, you're singing the rhythm of the hairta. This rudiment is quite common among drumset players, most notably in fills by drummers like Carter Beauford, Phil Collins, and Neil Peart. Tomas Haake even plays hairtas within grooves with his feet!

Technically speaking, the hairta is a simple rudiment to play. All of the strokes should be played as relaxed free strokes (aka full or legato strokes) where the sticks rebound back up by themselves, much like you're dribbling a basketball. The challenge is to play the strokes perfectly relaxed and with accurate rhythmic placement and good flow, especially when you move the rudiment to different parts of the beat and when you change lead hands.

Hairtas can be tricky because the two hands play different parts: One hand plays double strokes, and the other plays consistent single strokes. If you have good control of the single- and double-stroke roll, then your hands are trained with the necessary motions to execute the hairta. The challenge will be in the coordination and in understanding exactly what each hand should be doing.

The following exercises develop the hairta by separating the hands and applying the rudiment in different rhythmic locations in both triplet and duple frameworks. Make sure to play the double strokes consistently from

the check pattern into the hairta rudiment. When you add the hairta, the hand that plays the double strokes should not tighten up or change its rhythm or motion. You'll also want to check that the opposite hand is playing smooth and evenly spaced single strokes. The opposite hand's rhythm is often syncopated in an unusual way, but make sure it flows and plays evenly spaced notes nonetheless. Any tension or unevenness in that hand means you're working too hard and distorting the proper hairta rhythm. It's beneficial to play your right and left hand on different surfaces in order to clearly hear each hand's part.

Since hairtas come in sets of three partials, we can place the 24th- or 32nd-note rhythm behind the first, second, or third partial. The exercises contained here do this in both triplet and duple form. It's very important to play these exercises with a metronome while also tapping your foot so that you have a rhythmic point of reference. Without feeling the pulse beneath the complex rhythms of the hairta, you'll be developing only your hands and not your musical vocabulary. Once you're comfortable playing hairtas in unusual places rhythmically, try applying your new vocabulary on the drumset. If you practice diligently, it won't take long for this new rudiment and its many variations to pop up spontaneously within your playing. That's when all this rudimental training really pays off.

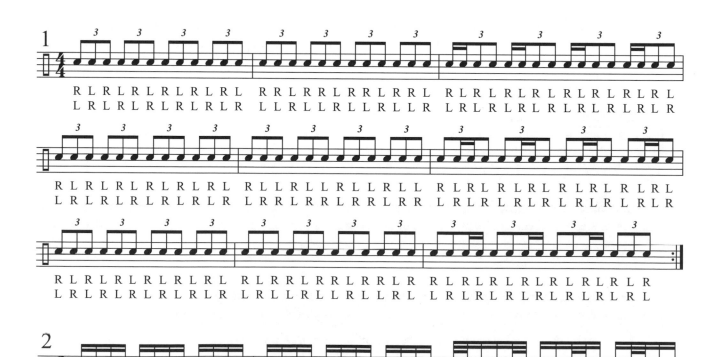

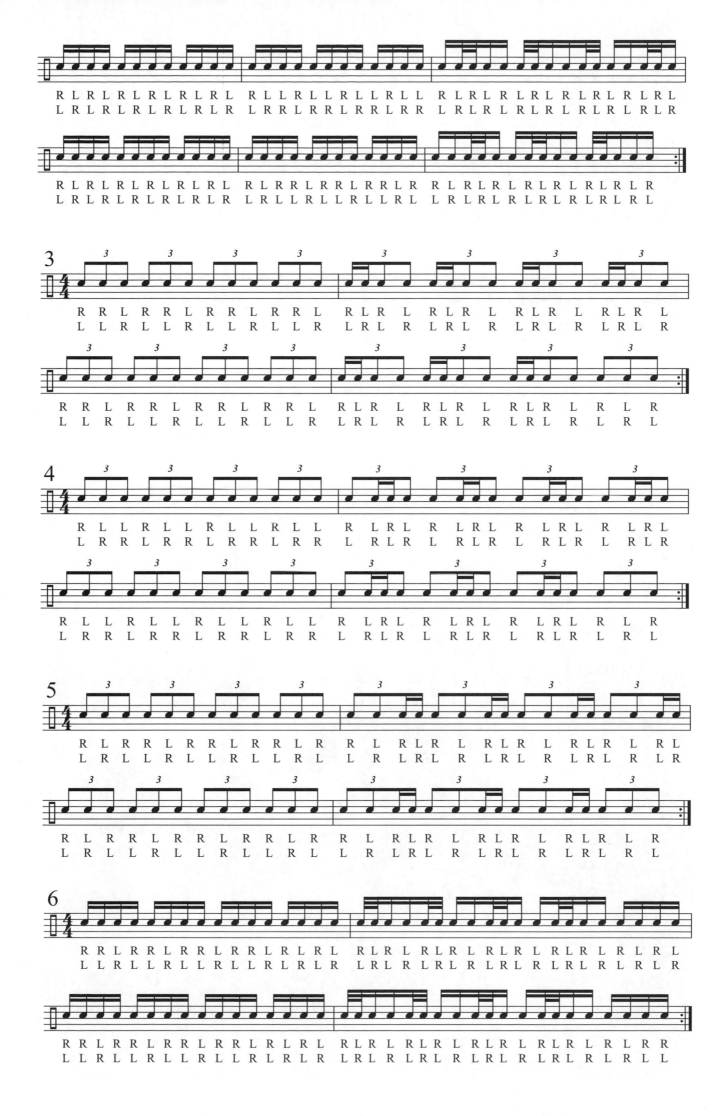

7

R L L R L L L R L L L R L L L R L R L   R L R L R L R L R L R L R L R L R L
L R R L R R R L R R R L R R R L R L R   L R L R L R L R L R L L L R L R L R

R L L R L L L R L L L R L L L R L R L   R L R L R L R L R L R L R L R L R R
L R R L R R R L R R R L R R R L R L R   L R L R L R L R L R L R L R L R L L

8

R L R R L R R L R R L R R L R R L R L   R L R L R L R L R L R L R L R L R L
L R L L R L L R L L R L L R L L R L R   L R L R L R L R L R L R L R L R L R

R L R R L R R L R R L R R L R R L R L   R L R L R L R L R L R L R L R L R R
L R L L R L L R L L R L L R L L R L R   L R L R L R L R L R L R L R L R L L

Sally Somers

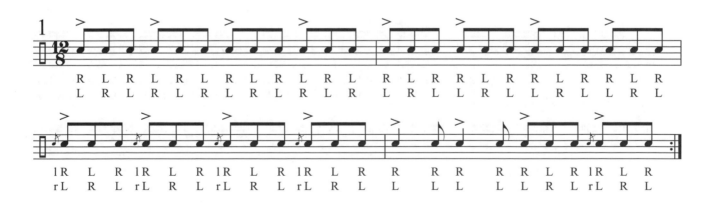

SAME-HAND FLAM ACCENT

In the Top Twelve Rudiments section, I covered alternating flam accents. When you play flam accents *without* alternating, they take on a new feel and require a different technique. The lead hand essentially plays a shuffle pattern, which requires a Moeller whip stroke. If you struggle or tighten up when playing fast shuffles, then this rudiment variation is for you!

Same-hand flam accents are not only great as a training tool for developing the inverted hand motion, they're also extremely useful when voiced around the drumkit.

The sticking for standard flam accents alternates. When you play flam accents back to back leading with the same hand, however, there's a low tap played immediately before the accent with the same hand. This is the inverted hand motion, a key technique that will serve you far beyond the context of this rudiment variation.

When you play same-hand flam accents slowly, it's very easy to use wrist strokes (free, down, up, and tap strokes) with exact stick heights for dynamic contrast. But at medium and faster tempos, there's not enough time for the wrist to perform an upstroke tap immediately before the accent. Forcing the issue will generally lead to tension in the wrist, while also dragging the tempo and creating a rhythmic gap before the accent. In this case, many slow repetitions will *not* lead to high speed, since the faster tempo requires a totally different technique. Because the wrist can no longer handle the demand at higher tempos, let's not use it.

At medium to fast tempos, it's time to let the forearm take over, by way of the Moeller whip-stroke technique. Now the wrist can just relax and enjoy the ride. The tap immediately preceding the accented flam will be played with a Moeller upstroke, where the stick hits the drum as you pick up the forearm and let the wrist hang limp. The forearm is then thrown down with the wrist relaxed so that the stick gets whipped toward the drum for the accent. The Moeller whip creates an accent, in part because of the slightly higher stick height, but mainly because of the higher velocity of the stroke.

At medium speeds, you may want to stifle the accent stroke's rebound in order to initiate the following tap. But at faster tempos where there's less time between each tap/accent combination, it's beneficial to let the accent stroke rebound. This way some of the accent's energy will flow into the next tap/accent combination so you don't have to start the process over from scratch. Keep in mind that if the flams are too wide, you'll need to whip the accent stroke with a faster forearm motion in order to get the stick to the drum sooner.

When you play the following exercises, be sure to coordinate the two hands so the flams sound consistent. Ideally, you want to be able to play these same-hand flam accents with flams that are very tight, wide and open, and everywhere in between. If you tighten up to stroke out the accent after the tap, then slow down to where you can play a relaxed and flowing whip stroke. (Tension will never develop into loose, flowing technique, no matter how many years you practice.) Play these exercises with a metronome or recorded music in order to train your hands with accurate timing and feel. Also be sure to practice leading with the left hand as well as the right.

PUH-DUH-DUH

This Chops Builder develops an incredibly useful stick-ing pattern called "puh-duh-duh," the name of which is onomatopoeia for the sticking RLL. We'll also invert the puh-duh-duh into the duh-duh-puh (RRL) for contrast. These combinations of three strokes may seem simple at first, but once you dig into them you'll find they're quite difficult to play accurately and with a loose and musical flow. Taking the time to master these stickings is worth the effort, since they're very expressive and handy when you're playing triplet feels. Jazz drummers use the stick-ings a lot in comping figures and in solo phrases.

The puh-duh-duh is a right-hand accent followed by two left taps. You're essentially playing triplets with an accent on the first partial. The inversion, duh-duh-puh, is two right-hand taps (or a low right-hand diddle) fol-lowed by a left-hand accent. This puts the accent on the third partial of the triplet. Using diddles instead of single strokes saves energy, and it also gives the triplets a dif-ferent feel. The puh-duh-duh should have a clear accent on the first note, and the two following taps should be played low to the drum with a light touch. The duh-duh-puh should get the same treatment, with a low and light diddle followed by a big accent.

It's important to have a firm grasp on the double-stroke roll before working on the puh-duh-duh, since one hand has to play double strokes. Be sure the doubles are played loosely, with the fingers smoothly rebounding the second stroke of the diddle. If the doubles are played as pure bounces with no finger reinforcement, they will sound weak. On the other hand, if the doubles are played as two forced wrist strokes, they will sound choked, and you'll also have limited potential for speed and flow. If your finger control is still a work in progress, err on the side of bouncy, since tight playing will never develop into finesse.

Once you can perform these exercises comfortably and with good technique, you'll find they lend themselves to very fast playing. Rudimentally savvy players may notice that when you play a puh-duh-duh and a duh-duh-puh back to back, it's actually a slurred six-stroke roll, or an inversion of the paradiddle-diddle. Get creative and com-bine these stickings in a variety of ways to say what you'd like to say musically. The combinations are a lot of fun on the kit too. Try moving the accents to different drums and cymbals and even playing some of the double strokes on the bass drum instead of the snare. There's a wealth of vocabulary built into these two vital stickings.

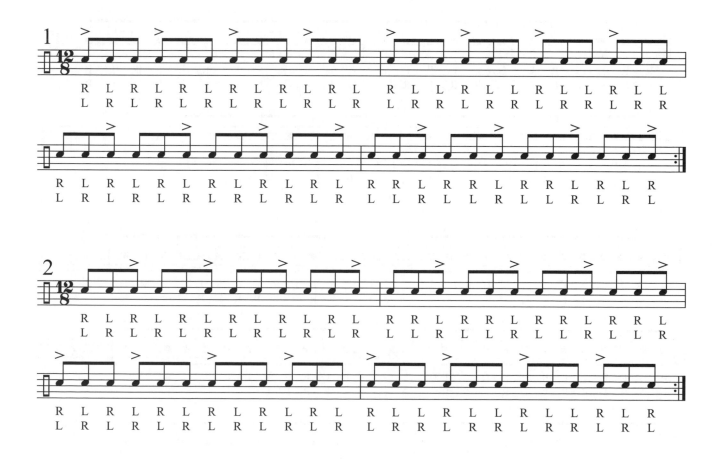

SINGLE FIVE

The single five isn't one of the Percussive Arts Society's standard forty, but it's a rudiment—and an extremely useful one at that. If you know how to play a five-stroke roll, then you have a head start on understanding the single five. It's the same rhythm, but with single strokes instead of double strokes. Beyond the sticking, the single five also stands apart in that it tends to sound fuller, it can be voiced around the kit in other ways, and it requires a different hand motion.

Technically speaking, the single five is a very simple rudiment to play. All of the strokes should be played as relaxed free strokes (aka full or legato strokes) where the sticks rebound much like a dribbling basketball. The challenge is to play the strokes perfectly relaxed with accurate rhythmic placement and good flow, especially when you move the rudiment to different positions rhythmically or when you change lead hands.

When we dissect the single five, we find the two hands play different parts: the lead hand plays triple strokes, while the opposite hand fills in with doubles. If you have good control of the triple- and double-stroke rolls, then your hands are trained with the necessary motions. The challenge is in the coordination and in understanding exactly what each hand does in order to properly apply those motions.

The following exercises develop single fives by separating the hands and isolating them in different rhythmic locations, in triplet and duple frameworks. The key is playing the triple strokes consistently from the check pattern into the single fives. When you add the double-stroke fill-in, the lead hand that plays the triple strokes should not tighten up or change its rhythm or motion. It's very important that every stroke of each single five is a true free stroke, where it rebounds smoothly to the "up" position. Be sure not to stop the last stroke, as in a downstroke, or it will be very difficult to develop speed with the single five. It's beneficial to play the hands on different surfaces, so you can hear the lead hand as it plays a relaxed and even rhythm.

It's very important to practice these exercises with a metronome and to tap your foot as a musical point of reference. These examples run the single fives through each possible rhythmic placement within triplet and duple form. Some placements will probably be familiar, while others may seem very strange. Go slowly and take the time to learn each placement thoroughly so that it starts to feel good. The better you understand these complex rhythms, the more music you can make.

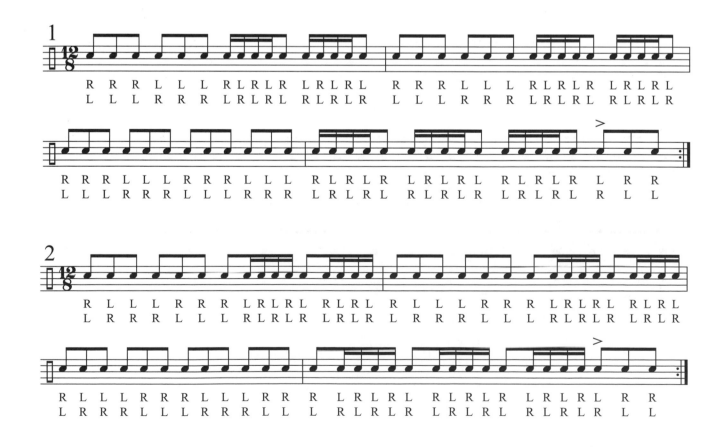

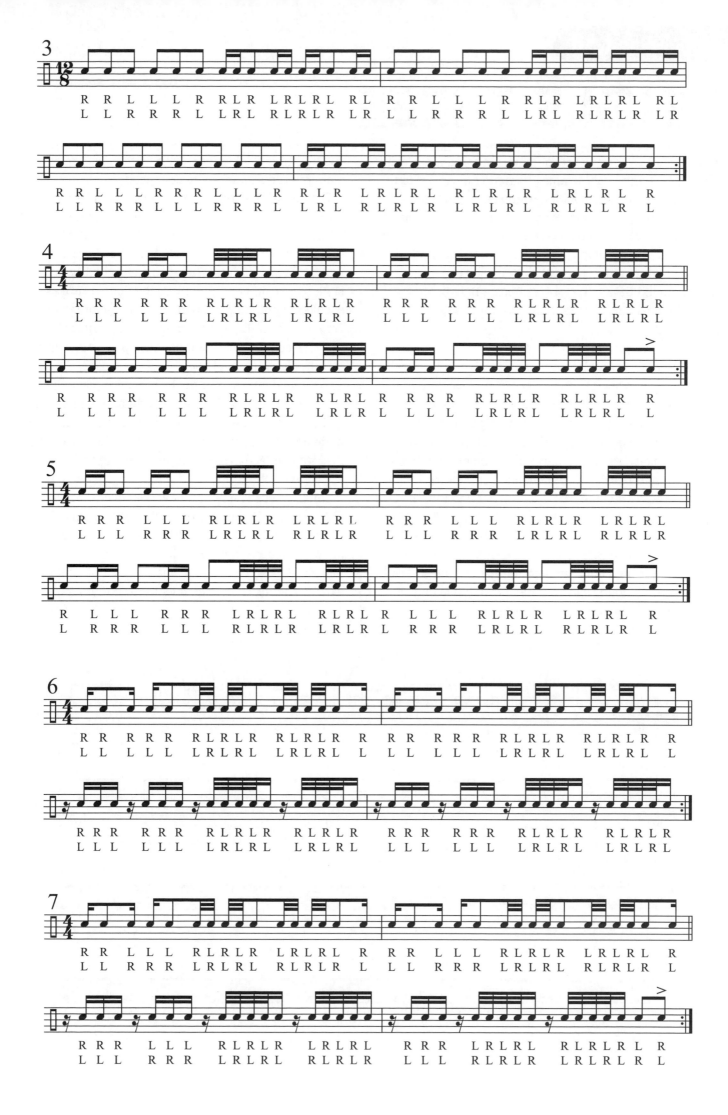

SINGLE THREE

The single three consists of groups of three notes, with the RLR and LRL stickings alternating back and forth. It's a great pattern for building even stick control from hand to hand, and it's also very beneficial for building double strokes once you see the bigger rhythm played by the lead hand. The single three can be used very creatively when put into different rhythmic placements and voiced around the drumkit. Drum heroes Billy Cobham, Simon Phillips, and Neil Peart have done this to great effect.

Technically speaking, the single three is a very simple rudiment to play. All of the strokes should be played as relaxed free strokes (aka full or legato strokes), where the sticks rebound by themselves much like a dribbling basketball. The challenge is to play the single three perfectly relaxed, with accurate rhythmic placement and good flow, especially when you move the rudiment to different positions rhythmically and/or change lead hands.

When you dissect the single three, you find that the lead hand plays a very familiar part: double strokes. If you have good control of the double-stroke roll, then it's just a matter of dropping in a note in the middle of the double with the opposite hand. The logic of this may be simple, but feeling the doubles in your hands while playing single threes is a different matter entirely. Once you're able to feel the doubles smoothly within the single threes,

you'll be able to play them with better sound quality, a more relaxed flow, and greater speed.

The following exercises develop single threes by separating the hands and isolating them in different rhythmic locations, in triplet and duple frameworks. Be sure to play the double strokes consistently from the check pattern into the single threes. When you add the fill-in single stroke, the lead hand that plays the double strokes shouldn't tighten up or change its rhythm or motion. It's very important that every stroke of each single three is a true free stroke, where it rebounds up smoothly and is instantly ready to play again. Since most of the exercises go from doubles to single threes, it's a good idea to practice playing the doubles on a drum or a pad and then add the inner beats on a different sound source. In doing this, you will be able to hear whether the doubles stay perfectly consistent when the inner beats are added.

Single threes will become even more challenging as we put them in different places rhythmically. Some placements will be familiar, while others may seem very strange. Practice these exercises with a metronome, and tap your foot so you have a musical point of reference. Go slowly, and take the time to learn each rhythmic placement thoroughly so you can play single threes with a good feel.

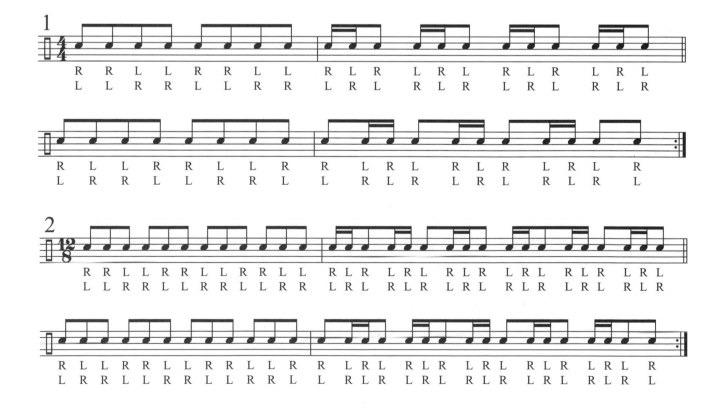

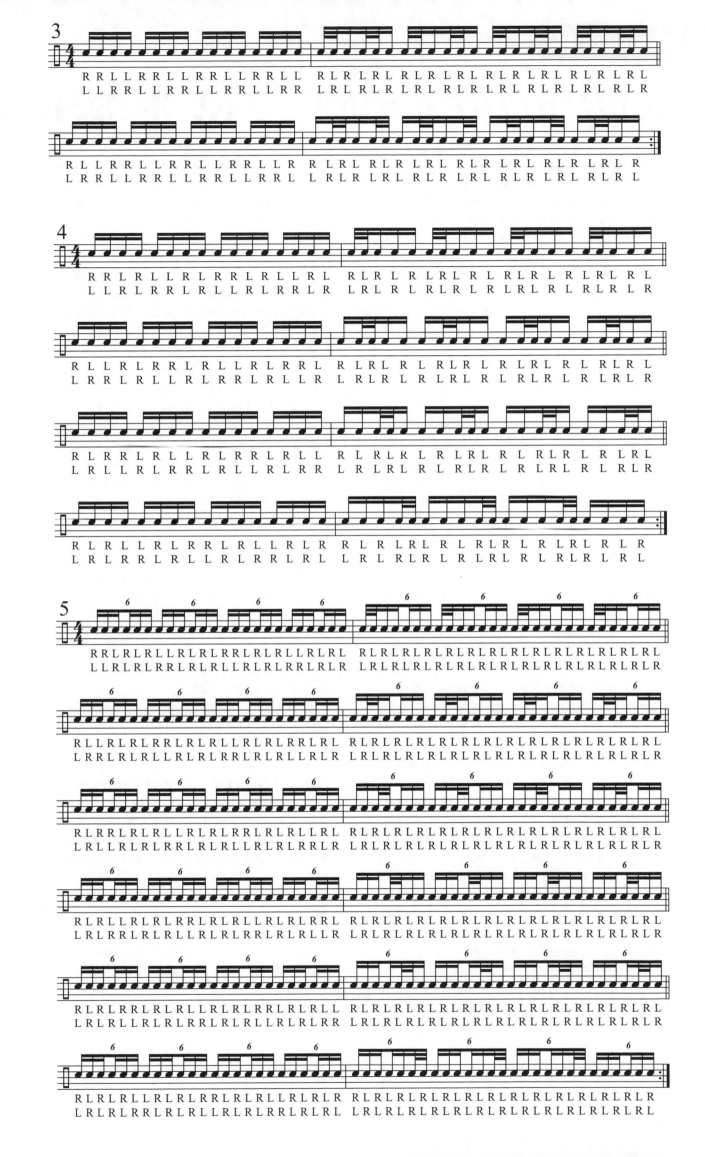

ACCENTS/TAPS: ADDED AND INTEGRATED

The ultimate accent/tap exercise is played with the various wrist-turn techniques—free strokes, downstrokes, tap strokes, and upstrokes. This is one of the most important exercises in the Chops Builders section, since your level of control in playing it is directly related to your ability to play any rudiment or sticking pattern containing accents and taps. The bottom line is this: The more control of accents and taps you have, the more music you can make on any single drum or cymbal, and the less reliant you'll be on using different instruments to create musical interest.

Let's begin by looking at each of the four wrist-turn techniques.

Free stroke (or full stroke): This is a simple dribble, where you throw the stick toward the drum, let it hit with all of its velocity, and then allow it to rebound—on its own accord—back up to where it started. This stroke should be made with a very loose grip so that the stick vibrates freely. The butt end of the stick should never hit the palm of your hand.

Tap stroke: This is essentially a low free stroke. Play tap strokes with a relaxed flow, and avoid squeezing the stick against the palm. Again, you should let the stick vibrate freely as your fingers do much of the finesse work.

Upstroke: This is basically a tap stroke where you lift the stick up after hitting the drum, in preparation for an accent. This stroke should also be made with a very loose grip so that the stick vibrates freely.

Downstroke: This starts as a free stroke, but immediately after hitting the drum the stick should be squeezed against the palm of the hand very briefly, in order to absorb the stick's energy and stop it low to the drum in preparation for a low tap.

When any accent/tap rudiment or pattern is executed perfectly, each stroke will be played with a smooth and relaxed technique, without the butt end of the stick being squeezed against the palm, except for the downstrokes.

There are two common errors that many drummers make when playing accent/tap patterns:

1. While playing the tap(s) after the downstroke, the stick is still held with the butt end squeezed against the palm. This is a common way of tightening up while playing, and it robs you of smooth sound quality, flow, speed, and endurance. It can also lead to injury.

2. The downstroke lacks the control to stop the stick at the lower height and flops somewhat out of control into the following taps. While it's certainly not as problematic as the first error, this incorrect way of playing leads to high, bouncy taps that lack dynamic contrast relative to the accents. Rhythmic accuracy is often sacrificed as well.

Since both of those common problems are related to the downstroke, let's talk a bit more about this technique. Remember that when you're playing anything with accents and taps, *downstrokes point down*.

In order for the downstroke to point down, the fulcrum of the drumstick must be held higher than the bead. The thumb should be on the topside of the stick, and there should be no gap between the thumb and first finger. This posture gives you some leverage, which is helpful in quickly squelching the stick's rebound. Plus it puts you in a position where the hand can drop down immediately after gripping the stick against the palm, in order for the fingers to open up and play taps freely. The challenge is to see how quickly the fingers can squeeze the stick against the palm to stop it and then relax and open up.

These exercises consist of groups of four notes played with zero, one, two, three, or four accents, plus various add-ins using the same patterns in the opposite hand. The fill-in hand will be added and taken away in different positions relative to the lead hand. The challenge is to coordinate the hands so that the lead hand remains perfectly consistent. (In the examples, T = tap, D = downstroke, U = upstroke, and F = free stroke. These strokes apply to the lead hand. When the opposing fill-in hand finishes playing in a given measure, it should end with a downstroke in order to rest low to the drum, in what is known as the "set" position.)

It's crucial to play the double stop, or unison, patterns flawlessly. (These are notated with a B in the examples.) Any flamming between the hands means they're not rhythmically accurate, which also means they won't alternate evenly. Flamming usually occurs when the two hands are not operating the same way technically. Be sure to watch your arms, hands, and stick heights, and try to create a mirror image when you play the double stops. It's important to play the repeats so that you also practice each pattern starting with the left. There are new mental challenges, as well as coordination issues to work through, when you lead with the opposite hand.

The more perfect repetitions you get, the more your muscle memory will lock in to playing correct and consistent rhythms. You will also have greater dynamic expression, and your sound quality will improve. Take your time to perfect this exercise, and the music will thank you.

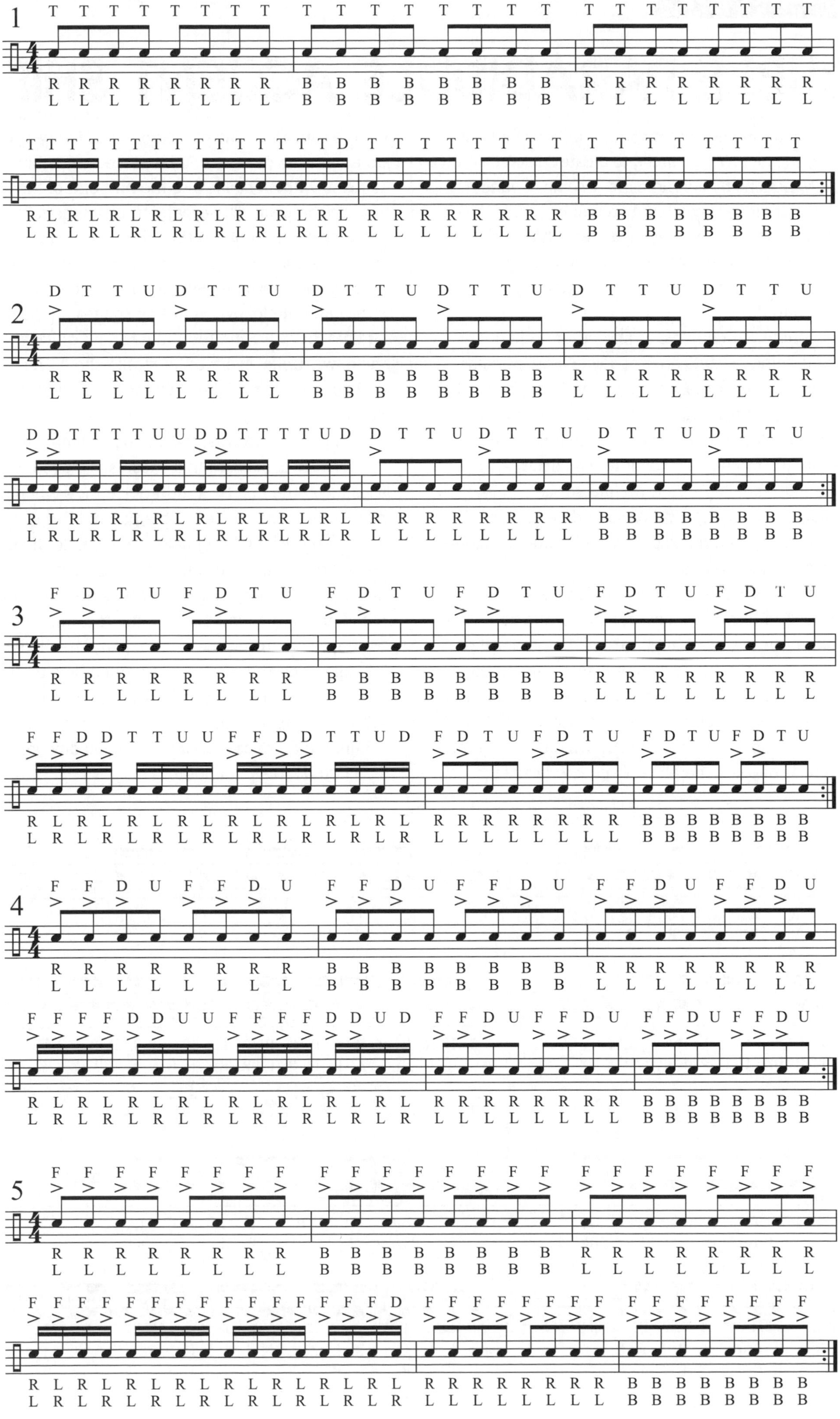
1
T T T T T T T T T T T T T T T T T T T T T T T T
R R R R R R R R B B B B B B B B R R R R R R R R
L L L L L L L L B B B B B B B B L L L L L L L L
T T T T T T T T T T T T T T T D T T T T T T T T T T T T T T T T
R L R L R L R L R L R L R L R L R R R R R R R R B B B B B B B B
L R L R L R L R L R L R L R L R L L L L L L L L B B B B B B B B
2
D T T U D T T U D T T U D T T U D T T U D T T U
R R R R R R R R B B B B B B B B R R R R R R R R
L L L L L L L L B B B B B B B B L L L L L L L L
D D T T T T U U D D T T T T U D D T T U D T T U D T T U D T T U
R L R L R L R L R L R L R L R L R R R R R R R R B B B B B B B B
L R L R L R L R L R L R L R L R L L L L L L L L B B B B B B B B
3
F D T U F D T U F D T U F D T U F D T U F D T U
R R R R R R R R B B B B B B B B R R R R R R R R
L L L L L L L L B B B B B B B B L L L L L L L L
F F D D T T U U F F D D T T U D F D T U F D T U F D T U F D T U
R L R L R L R L R L R L R L R L R R R R R R R R B B B B B B B B
L R L R L R L R L R L R L R L R L L L L L L L L B B B B B B B B
4
F F D U F F D U F F D U F F D U F F D U F F D U
R R R R R R R R B B B B B B B B R R R R R R R R
L L L L L L L L B B B B B B B B L L L L L L L L
F F F F D D U U F F F F D D U D F F D U F F D U F F D U F F D U
R L R L R L R L R L R L R L R L R R R R R R R R B B B B B B B B
L R L R L R L R L R L R L R L R L L L L L L L L B B B B B B B B
5
F F F F F F F F F F F F F F F F F F F F F F F F
R R R R R R R R B B B B B B B B R R R R R R R R
L L L L L L L L B B B B B B B B L L L L L L L L
F F F F F F F F F F F F F F F D F F F F F F F F F F F F F F F F
R L R L R L R L R L R L R L R L R R R R R R R R B B B B B B B B
L R L R L R L R L R L R L R L R L L L L L L L L B B B B B B B B

DOUBLE PARADIDDLE ACCENT SHIFTER

The standard double paradiddle has only one accent, on the first beat. We're going to create some musically applicable variations by adding more accents in various places. Not every accent combination will be represented in this article. The ones I've included were chosen because they will quickly manifest themselves in your playing around the drumkit, plus they make for a rich study in accent/tap control.

To play double paradiddles, or any other rudiment or pattern containing accents and taps, you'll need to use the four basic strokes: free, down, up, and tap. Remember that the free stroke is a high stroke that ends high by allowing the stick to rebound back up freely. The downstroke is a high stroke that ends low. The upstroke is a low stroke that ends high. And the tap stroke is a low stroke that stays low. Tap strokes should be played as low free strokes with a relaxed flow and without squeezing the stick against the palm.

A downstroke or an upstroke should be used when there's a need to play the following stroke at a new stick height. When there's no change in stick height for the following note, a free stroke (sometimes in the form of a tap) should be played. Your goal should be to play free strokes as often as possible, in order to play as loosely as you can. You should play downstrokes only when the following note needs to be played at a low tap height.

Here's another way of looking at it: Every stroke within an accent/tap pattern will be played smoothly and relaxed, without squeezing the butt end of the stick against the palm. The exception is downstrokes, where we very briefly squeeze the stick's butt end against the palm in order to stop the stick at a lower height. The key is to achieve absolute separation between the downstroke and the following tap by squeezing the stick against the palm and then releasing it quickly. Aside from the downstroke, every other stroke should remain relaxed and flowing, so that the stick resonates within a loose hand.

Let's get started with the standard double paradiddle. We want to make sure that these are played with clear accents on the first beat; otherwise they will have a monotone sound. If the double paradiddles sound dynamically expressive when played on a single drum, then adding the different colors of the drumset will be that much more exciting. The six strokes played in the double paradiddle are down, tap, tap, up, tap, tap, with the last two taps comprising the diddle. (Play the diddle with a low alley-oop/drop-catch technique.) Be sure that every stroke other than the initial downstroke is played with relaxed hands and that the sticks flow freely.

Here are three exercises to help you develop the standard double paradiddle.

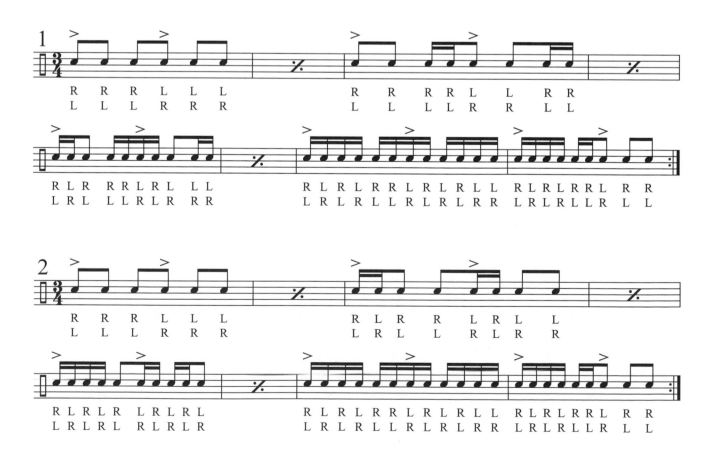

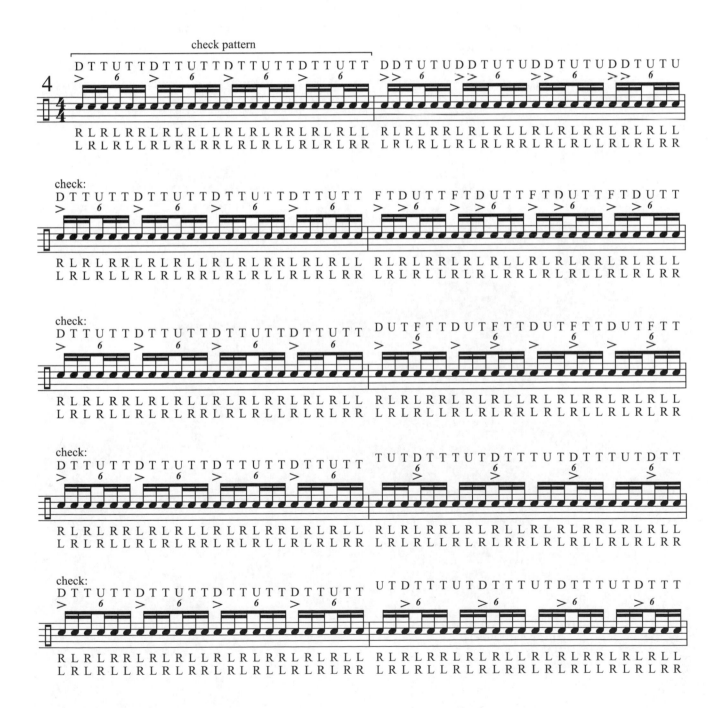

3

| R | L | L | R | R | L | L | R | | RLRLLRLRRLRLLRLR | | | R | L | L | R | R | L | L | R |
| L | R | R | L | L | R | R | L | | LRLRRLRLLRLRRLRL | | | L | R | R | L | L | R | R | L |

| R | L | R | R | L | R | L | L | R | L | R | R | L | R | L | L | | R | L | L | R | R | L | L | R | | RLRLRRLRLRLLRLRLRRLRLR |
| L | R | L | L | R | L | R | R | L | R | L | L | R | L | R | R | | L | R | R | L | L | R | R | L | | LRLRLLRLRLRRLRLRLLRLRL |

Now that we've covered the standard double paradiddle, let's check out some double paradiddle accent variations. (Note that over each beat the stroke type is defined, with an F for free stroke, a D for downstroke, a T for tap stroke, or a U for upstroke.) Play the variations very slowly at first, making sure that each stroke type is played accurately. Check that every free stroke rebounds freely, that every downstroke stops with the stick clearly pointing down toward the drum, and that the taps and upstrokes are played with a relaxed flow within a loose hand.

4

check pattern

D T T U T T D T T U T T D T T U T T D T T U T T | D D T U T U D D T U T U D D T U T U D D T U T U

| R | L | R | L | R | R | L | R | L | R | L | L | R | L | R | L | R | R | L | R | L | R | L | L | | R | L | R | L | R | R | L | R | L | R | L | L | R | L | R | L | R | R | L | R | L | R | L | L |
| L | R | L | R | L | L | R | L | R | L | R | R | L | R | L | R | L | L | R | L | R | L | R | R | | L | R | L | R | L | L | R | L | R | L | R | R | L | R | L | R | L | L | R | L | R | L | R | R |

check:
D T T U T T D T T U T T D T T U T T D T T U T T | F T D U T T F T D U T T F T D U T T F T D U T T

| R | L | R | L | R | R | L | R | L | R | L | L | R | L | R | L | R | R | L | R | L | R | L | L | | R | L | R | L | R | R | L | R | L | R | L | L | R | L | R | L | R | R | L | R | L | R | L | L |
| L | R | L | R | L | L | R | L | R | L | R | R | L | R | L | R | L | L | R | L | R | L | R | R | | L | R | L | R | L | L | R | L | R | L | R | R | L | R | L | R | L | L | R | L | R | L | R | R |

check:
D T T U T T D T T U T T D T T U T T D T T U T T | D U T F T T D U T F T T D U T F T T D U T F T T

| R | L | R | L | R | R | L | R | L | R | L | L | R | L | R | L | R | R | L | R | L | R | L | L | | R | L | R | L | R | R | L | R | L | R | L | L | R | L | R | L | R | R | L | R | L | R | L | L |
| L | R | L | R | L | L | R | L | R | L | R | R | L | R | L | R | L | L | R | L | R | L | R | R | | L | R | L | R | L | L | R | L | R | L | R | R | L | R | L | R | L | L | R | L | R | L | R | R |

check:
D T T U T T D T T U T T D T T U T T D T T U T T | T U T D T T T U T D T T T U T D T T T U T D T T

| R | L | R | L | R | R | L | R | L | R | L | L | R | L | R | L | R | R | L | R | L | R | L | L | | R | L | R | L | R | R | L | R | L | R | L | L | R | L | R | L | R | R | L | R | L | R | L | L |
| L | R | L | R | L | L | R | L | R | L | R | R | L | R | L | R | L | L | R | L | R | L | R | R | | L | R | L | R | L | L | R | L | R | L | R | R | L | R | L | R | L | L | R | L | R | L | R | R |

check:
D T T U T T D T T U T T D T T U T T D T T U T T | U T D T T T U T D T T T U T D T T T U T D T T T

| R | L | R | L | R | R | L | R | L | R | L | L | R | L | R | L | R | R | L | R | L | R | L | L | | R | L | R | L | R | R | L | R | L | R | L | L | R | L | R | L | R | R | L | R | L | R | L | L |
| L | R | L | R | L | L | R | L | R | L | R | R | L | R | L | R | L | L | R | L | R | L | R | R | | L | R | L | R | L | L | R | L | R | L | R | R | L | R | L | R | L | L | R | L | R | L | R | R |

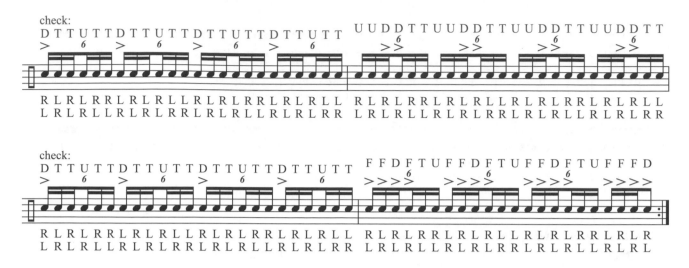

Practice perfect repetitions of each rudiment variation by playing along with a metronome or recorded music at an appropriate tempo. Play the variations no faster than the top speed at which you can execute them perfectly and comfortably. Stay at this tempo for as long as twenty minutes, and then bump up the tempo about ten beats a minute and repeat. You will see better results by taking this more patient approach. When drummers practice only at the edge of their fastest tempos, they're almost always doing so at the expense of proper technique. Plus they're developing improper muscle memory, which will be hard to unlearn later.

R L R R R L L R L R R L
L R L L R R L R L L R R

PARADIDDLE-DIDDLE AND EXTENSIONS

The paradiddle-diddle is a standard rudiment, and it's a great one to know because it has many applications for being voiced around the drumkit. It also features a key motion in the lead hand, which will greatly benefit swing and broken-up triplet patterns. By adding more diddles to the paradiddle-diddle, we can creatively apply this rudiment to any accent pattern. To do this, we apply the "para" sticking to the accent and then fill in the spaces between the accents with however many diddles are needed. It's very effective to play the "para" accent on the toms or with a crash cymbal/bass drum unison while filling in diddles on the snare. There's a lot of music to be made with this rudiment and its variations.

First let's look at the technique necessary to play the paradiddle-diddle. At slow to medium tempos the lead hand plays a downstroke accent, where the stick stops low to the drum and points down toward the drumhead. It's important to quickly stop the stick low in order for it to get a fresh start in playing the following relaxed and low unaccented diddle. The low diddles should be played with the alley-oop/drop-catch technique at a low stick height. The opposite hand simply plays low taps, which requires good finger control. (Note that the paradiddle-diddle has separate parts played by each hand and does not alternate, so it's very important to practice it leading with each hand.) With the exception of the accented downstroke, which requires a bit of energy, the hands should be very relaxed for the other strokes, and the sticks should vibrate freely.

As you increase the tempo, it's okay to let the accent stroke rebound a bit more so that some of its energy flows into the following diddle. But do your best to maintain a clear accent so that the dynamic contrast remains intact. When you play paradiddle-diddles very fast, there's no longer enough time to play an upstroke in preparation for the accent. Now it's time to use the Moeller whip-stroke combination, which uses arms instead of wrists for the accents and allows the stick's energy to flow from the accent into the following diddle. It may help to think about whipping the accent and then letting the stick flop into the diddle. When you employ this technique, the wrist is not as involved and the fingers help out by playing the second beat of the diddle. The accent will still be clear because of the greater velocity of the whip stroke, even while the next diddle is played at almost the same stick height.

The following exercises work the paradiddle-diddle on the downbeat and then on the upbeat. Then we have some variations with extra diddles filling in the spaces. Finally, we'll take the four most common clave patterns and apply the paradiddle-diddle to them.

Perform the following exercises with the correct stickings, use a metronome (or play along with your favorite tunes), be sure to practice with each hand leading, and don't go any faster than you can play comfortably. When the tempo reaches the limit of your abilities, it's better to play a bit weak and bouncy than to try to stroke everything out. By all means, avoid tightening your technique and forcing the accents and diddles.

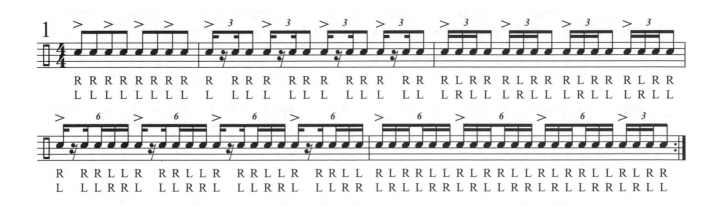

1

R R R R R R R   R   R R R   R R R   R R R   R R   R L R R   R L R R   R L R R   R L R R
L L L L L L L L   L   L L L   L L L   L L L   L L   L R L L   L R L L   L R L L   L R L L

R   R R L L R   R R L L R   R R L L R   R R L L   R L R R L L R L R R L L R L R R L L R L R R
L   L L R R L   L L R R L   L L R R L   L L R R   L R L L R R L R L L R R L R L L R R L R L L

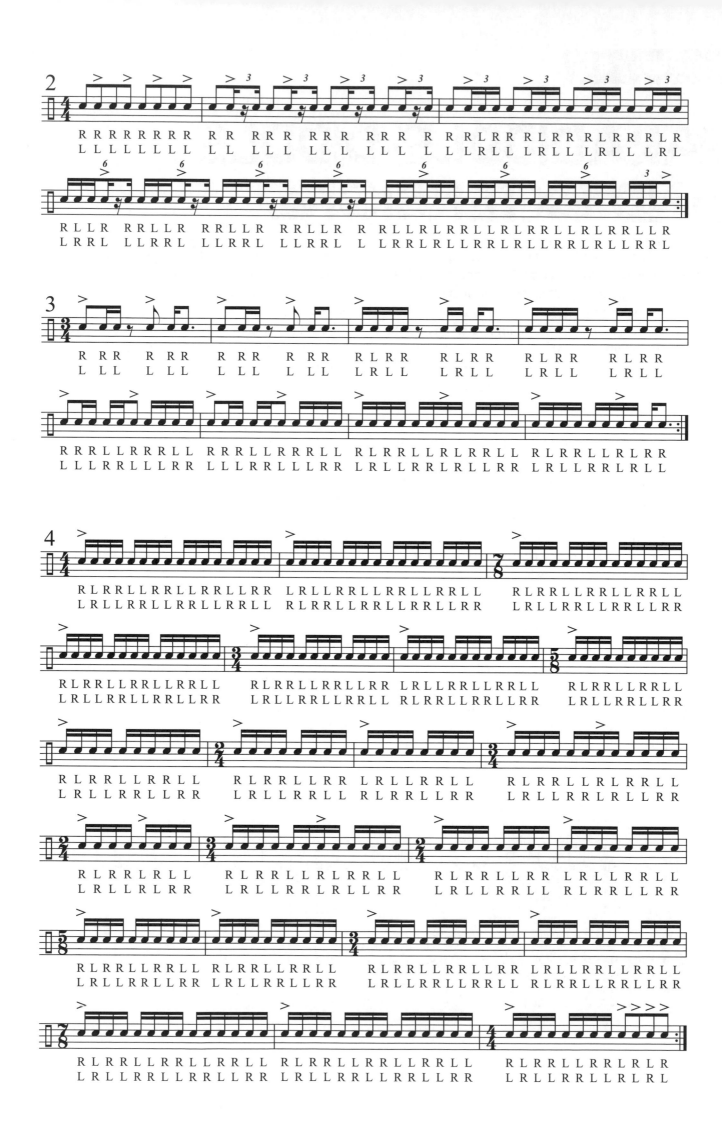

3:2 son clave

5

```
R L R R L L R L R R L L R L R R   L L R R L R L L R L R R L L R R
L R L L R R L R L L R R L R L L   R R L L R L R R L R L L R R L L
```

2:3 son clave

6

```
R R L L R L R R L R L L R R L L   R L R R L L R L R R L L R L R R
L L R R L R L L R L R R L L R R   L R L L R R L R L L R R L R L L
```

3:2 rumba clave

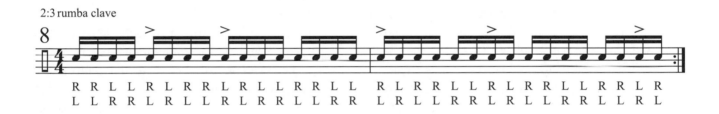

7

```
R L R R L L R L R R L L R R L R   L L R R L R L L R L R R L L R R
L R L L R R L R L L R R L L R L   R R L L R L R R L R L L R R L L
```

2:3 rumba clave

8

```
R R L L R L R R L R L L R R L L   R L R R L L R L R R L L R R L R
L L R R L R L L R L R R L L R R   L R L L R R L R L L R R L L R L
```

INVERTED STICKING PATTERNS WITH SINGLE-STROKE FILL-INS

An inverted sticking is any sticking where a tap, or series of taps, immediately precedes an accent with the same hand. Because at most tempos there's almost no time for the wrist to perform an upstroke, the accent will need to be played with a Moeller whip stroke. The stickings and single-stroke patterns presented in the exercises here are not only great training tools for developing the key inverted hand motion, but they're also extremely useful when voiced around the drumkit. Once you've worked through these exercises, you should be able to apply the inverted sticking and fill-in concept to any accent pattern you choose.

When playing these inverted stickings slowly, it's easy to use wrist strokes (free strokes, downstrokes, upstrokes, and tap strokes) with clearly defined high and low stick heights for maximum dynamic contrast. But when you play the stickings at a medium tempo and faster, there's not enough time for the wrist to perform an upstroke tap before hitting the accent. Forcing the issue will generally lead to tension in the wrist that can potentially cause injury. Plus you'll end up dragging the tempo and leaving a little rhythmic gap before the accent. (This is a perfect example of an instance where slow repetitions will not lead to higher speed, because the faster tempo requires a totally different technique.)

Since the wrist can no longer handle the demand of these inverted stickings at faster tempos, let's not use it. Instead, we'll let the forearm take over by employing the Moeller whip-stroke technique. Now the wrist can relax and enjoy the ride, instead of gumming up the works. The tap immediately preceding the accent will be played with a Moeller upstroke, where the stick just happens to hit the drum as you pick up the forearm and let the hand and stick hang limp. (Be sure not to start lifting the forearm any

sooner than the final tap preceding the accent.) The forearm is then thrown down and the wrist remains relaxed, so that the hand and stick get whipped toward the drum for the accent.

The Moeller whip stroke creates an accent in part because of the slightly higher stick height that it creates, but mainly because of the higher velocity of the stroke. In this context, each Moeller whip-stroke accent will need to be played as a Moeller downstroke so that the bead of the stick is stopped low to the drumhead in order to play the following low tap.

The fill-ins in the exercises are the notes that the opposite hand plays in the holes within the leading hand's inverted sticking. Fill-ins are simple to add, and the resulting single-stroke patterns sound impressively fast. The key is to think about the hands independently so that you can focus primarily on the leading hand's part. No matter what your hands are playing, applying this independence thought process will often result in the ability to play things much faster and more comfortably, since it allows you to think about half as much information.

The following exercises break down inverted stickings in groups of four, three, and two notes and then move into patterns that have two accents played back to back. I've also plugged inverted stickings into 3:2 and 2:3 son clave rhythms. Be sure to stay loose, and don't push the tempos faster than you can play comfortably. If you tighten up to stroke out the accent after the tap, be sure to slow down the tempo to a point where you can play a relaxed and flowing Moeller whip stroke. Tension will never develop in loose, flowing technique—no matter how many years you practice! Finally, play the exercises with a metronome or recorded music in order to develop accurate timing and a solid feel. And be sure to practice all of the exercises starting with the left hand too.

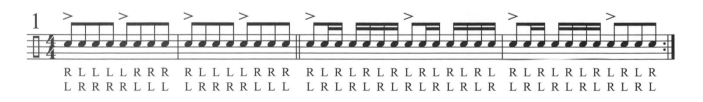

SWISS ARMY TRIPLET

The Swiss Army triplet rudiment offers you the opportunity to play groups of three notes with a flam at the beginning in such a way that each hand plays only doubles. It might sound as if there's a lot going on, but it's physically pretty easy to play. The Swiss Army triplet has built-in dynamics, flows extremely well, and is very useful for making music around the kit in both straight-8th and triplet forms. When you listen to Tony Williams blazing flam patterns on his toms, quite often they're simply Swiss triplets.

The key to the Swiss triplet is the double beat played by the lead hand. The double should be played in such a way that the two strokes decrescendo without the stick stopping (no-chop flop-and-drop). When going from the accent to the tap, we would normally play a downstroke and stop the stick low to the drum in order to achieve dynamic contrast. In this case, however, at even a medium tempo there isn't enough time to stop the stick after the accent and then restart it for the tap at a lower height. Therefore we need to allow the lead hand to play a freely rebounding double where the second stroke is an intentionally weak bounce. This free rebound creates the dynamic contrast between the accent and tap, and it allows the stick's energy from the initial accent to flow into the inner beat.

The opposite hand will need to play the grace note and third partial of the triplet. These two notes form a low double, which will require some finger control and finesse. In regular flams, the grace note should be pushed ahead rhythmically in order to precede the following hand's accent. But in Swiss triplets, the double beats are straightened out into an even double in order to flow smoothly. The flam between the two hands is created by laying back the accent just behind the grace note.

Swiss triplets should feel as if you're playing weak doubles with the lead hand and filling in the gaps with the opposite hand. For those of you with well-developed "alley-oop" finger control for playing strong double beats (where both beats are at roughly the same stick height and dynamic level), avoid using too much of these chops, as strong inner beats will diminish the impact of the accent in Swiss triplets. The more you can exaggerate the contrast in stick height and dynamics, the better, since your goal is to emulate an accented flam and an unaccented tap.

Here are quick tips for playing Swiss Army triplets:

1. Avoid hitting the accents extra hard with tight strokes, where the fingers are squeezing the stick when they should be playing the second note of the double.

2. Avoid letting the accent bounce up high, leaving you unable to differentiate the dynamic between the accent and tap.

3. Play the first stroke with a big accent from a high stick height. Don't cheat the accent in the interest of playing the following beats low.

When you practice Swiss triplets from slow to fast to slow over one minute, the slow speed will require a slightly different technique. At very slow tempos, all of the strokes can easily be played with the wrists, using downstrokes on the accents for clear dynamic contrast. As you get to a medium speed and higher, you'll need to start letting the stick bounce loosely from the accent to the second and third beats, or else the wrists will tighten up. This change in technique should happen gradually, in correlation with the tempo.

Practice the following exercises slowly, and then begin to work your way up in tempo. Since Swiss triplets don't alternate, be sure to practice them leading with each hand.

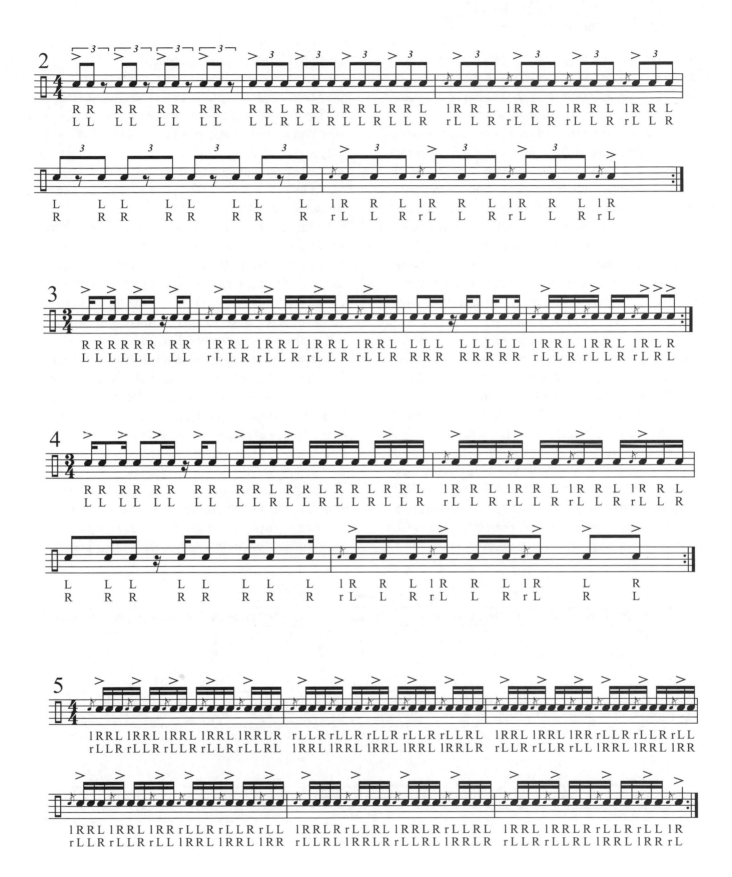

IRISH SPRING

ow we're going to go old school—with a new twist. What we're working on is a standard exercise called "Irish Spring" that comprises swung double beats with smooth hand-to-hand turnarounds.

This exercise has been used by rudimental drummers for decades, but here we're going to add a tag (ending) and experiment with some fill-ins. This exercise, when practiced correctly, will not only do wonders for your finger control (which is necessary to play relaxed and powerful alley-oop doubles), but will also help your shuffle feel become smoother than ever.

The best technique to use for each note in these exercises is the free stroke. (The free stroke is where you throw the stick down toward the drum with your wrist and fingers, allow it to hit the drum with all of its velocity, and then let it rebound back up on its own—just like dribbling a basketball.) If the second stroke of a double doesn't rebound all the way back up on its own, that means there was either extra tension in your hand inhibiting the stick's flow or the second beat of the double was too weak to bounce back up on its own. Underdeveloped doubles are generally stiffly stroked or weakly bounced. The free stroke will help ensure that both strokes of the double are played with high velocity and loose, relaxed hands. The beauty of free strokes is that they work only when played perfectly. If you feel as if you're not working very hard, then you're probably playing the free strokes correctly.

Even at moderate speeds it's unrealistic for the wrist to play both strokes with the exact same technique, so we'll employ the alley-oop technique. In the alley-oop technique, the first stroke is higher and slower and is played mainly with the wrist. The second stroke is lower and is played mainly with the fingers at a higher velocity. Think of the first stroke of the double as a setup for the second stroke.

Adding a slight accent to the second stroke helps build the finger control necessary to play smooth, open doubles. In most contexts, the second beat of the double falls on an upbeat instead of a downbeat. The beauty of the Irish Spring exercise is that it's in 12/8, so the second beat of the doubles falls on the downbeats, which is where the accents would fall naturally.

Irish Spring is structured in a common 4-2-1 format where you play something four times, then two times (and repeat), then one time (and repeat four times). There's a two-bar turnaround at the end that allows you to repeat the exercise leading with the opposite hand. The first bar of the turnaround contains 8th notes played as doubles, and the second bar is the same rhythm with an inverted double-stroke sticking. Make sure you tap your foot and feel the pulse throughout. (The exercises are written in 12/8 to make them easier to read, but they can also be interpreted as 8th-note triplets.)

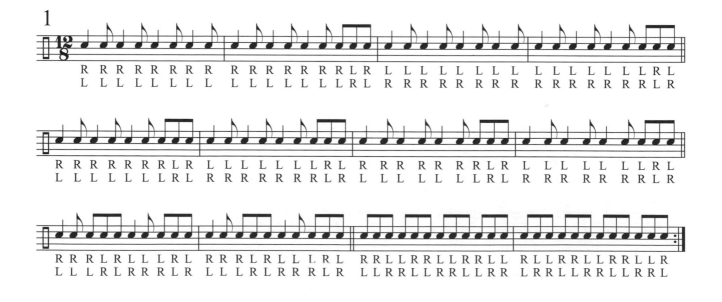

Now we're going to fill in the missing 8th notes with the opposite hand. This leaves us with constant 8th notes that should flow the whole way through. The challenge is to make it sound perfectly steady with no rhythmic hiccups and no accidental dynamic changes due to inconsistent doubles.

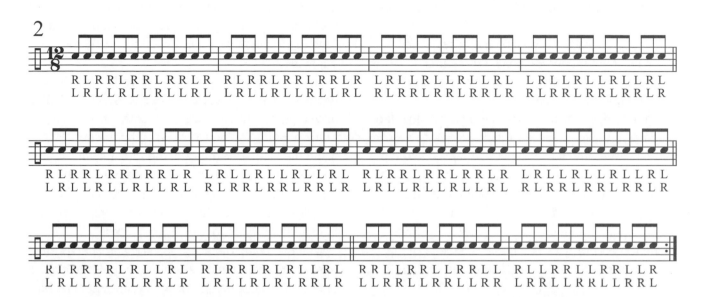

2

R L R R L R R L R R L R R L R R L R R L R R L R L R L L R L L R L L R L L R L L R L L R L L R L
L R L L R L L R L L R L L R L L R L L R L L R L R L R R L R R L R R L R R L R R L R R L R R L R

R L R R L R R L R R L R L R L L R L L R L L R L R L R R L R R L R R L R L R L L R L L R L L R L
L R L L R L L R L L R L R L R R L R R L R R L R L R L L R L L R L L R L R L R R L R R L R R L R

R L R R L R L R L L R L R L R R L R L R L L R L R R L L R R L L R R L L R L L R L L R R L L R
L R L L R L R L R R L R L R L L R L R L R R L R L L R R L L R R L L R R L R R L L R R L L R R L

IRISH SPRING WITH ACCENTS

For our final Chops Builder, we're going to add accents and taps to Irish Spring. These variations require a different technique in order to be played correctly.

When you get these exercises dialed in with the maximum stick height and dynamic differential between the accents and taps, your shuffle feel on the drumset will greatly improve.

In the following exercises, each hand plays a low tap that's immediately followed by a high accent. At a slow tempo, you can easily play an upstroke for the low tap and a downstroke for the accent using the wrist. But if you try to play at a medium or fast speed using that same technique, your wrists will seize up because there's not enough time for them to play an upstroke preceding the accent. This is where the Moeller whip downstroke (whip-and-stop) technique comes into play.

When drummers hear the name Moeller, they usually think of a looping three-note accent/tap/tap pattern. I call that the Moeller whip-stroke combination, or the whip-and-flop technique. While it's useful to know how to play that pattern, it's only one example of what's possible when employing the Moeller technique.

A Moeller stroke is a stroke using a whiplike motion. After the whip, you have the option to flop into a tap immediately following the accent, or you can stop the stick when there's time after the accent preceding the next low tap. Whip-and-flop and whip-and-stop each has appropriate applications, so you should have command of both.

The following exercises are best played using the Moeller whip-and-stop technique so that you can replace the wrist's motion with a forearm motion and then stop the stick so that it points slightly down with the bead about 1" off the head. This whipping motion from the forearm allows the wrist to simply relax and enjoy the ride.

The next note should be played with a Moeller upstroke where the stick just happens to hit the drum as you pick up the forearm and let the wrist hang limp. Think about dragging the stick up by the arm. When using the Moeller technique, the forearm should always be the first thing to move, while the bead of the stick is the last. After playing the Moeller upstroke, you're back in the "up" position with the hand and stick hanging limp and are ready to repeat the process.

When you play the exercises at faster speeds, the forearm motion should get smaller in order to conserve energy. The stick height for the accent will now be achieved in part by the whipping motion and also by the palm of the hand bumping the butt end of the stick down, which consequently pops up the bead. Regardless of tempo, be sure to quickly stifle the stick's rebound after the accent in order to freeze the stick pointing down toward the drum so that it's ready for the next low tap. The greater the stick height differential between the accents and taps, the greater the dynamic contrast.

Since all of the notes in the two-bar turnaround are accented, they should be played using smooth, rebounding free strokes. This will serve as a refreshing break from the Moeller whip-and-stop downstrokes used in the remainder of the exercise.

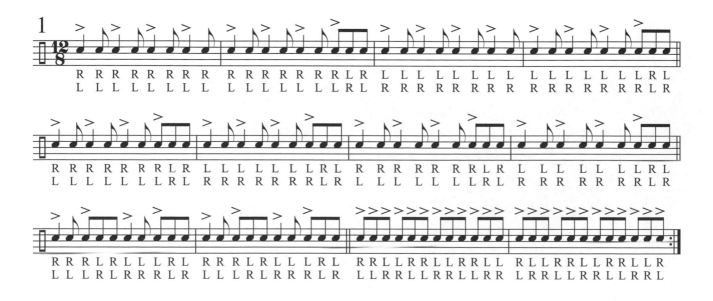

Now play the same exercise while filling in the missing 8th notes with the opposite hand. Make sure the entire exercise sounds perfectly steady with no rhythmic hiccups and no accidental dynamic shifts caused by inconsistent accent/tap stick heights or changes in stroke velocity.

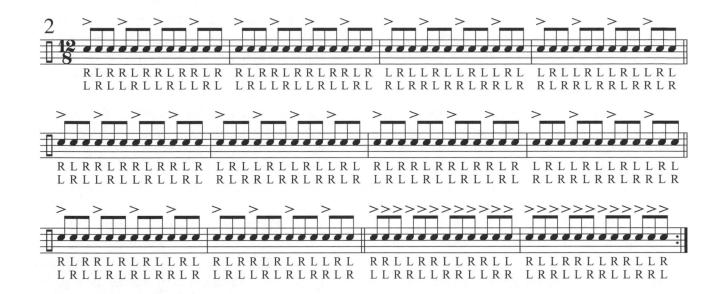

RLRRLRRLRRLR   RLRRLRRLRRLR   LRLLRLLRLLRL   LRLLRLLRLLRL
LRLLRLLRLLRL   LRLLRLLRLLRL   RLRRLRRLRRLR   RLRRLRRLRRLR

RLRRLRRLRRLR   LRLLRLLRLLRL   RLRRLRRLRRLR   LRLLRLLRLLRL
LRLLRLLRLLRL   RLRRLRRLRRLR   LRLLRLLRLLRL   RLRRLRRLRRLR

RLRRLRLRLLRL   RLRRLRLRLLRL   RRLLRRLLRRLL   RLLRRLLRRLLR
LRLLRLRLRRLR   LRLLRLRLRRLR   LLRRLLRRLLRR   LRRLLRRLLRRL

8TH-NOTE RIDE

To conclude *Stick Technique* we're going to look at a few coordination exercises starting with one where the two hands play fourteen basic 8th- and 16th-note patterns in duple meter, with different techniques and motions utilized in each hand. Playing these types of patterns is commonly referred to as employing independence, but it's really more a matter of coordination, or "coordinative interdependence."

The right hand (the hand that you most often use on the hi-hat and ride cymbal) will play 8th notes with accents on the downbeats, using a Moeller whip-and-flop motion, while the opposite hand will play the fourteen basic rhythms using free strokes initiated from the wrist. This may seem simple at first, but flowing and staying completely relaxed with each hand using a different technique is easier said than done. The key is to coordinate the hands so that each is seemingly unaware of what the other is doing—yet the two are playing together perfectly. Mastering these fourteen two-hand combinations will leave you with a better groove, stronger time, and an increased vocabulary.

First let's look at the lead hand. Rather than playing straight 8th notes at a perfectly uniform volume level, put an accent on the downbeats in order to groove harder. To make this accent/tap pattern flow as naturally as possible, apply the Moeller whip-and-flop technique in place of the usual wrist-oriented downstroke/upstroke combination. The accents will be whipped from the forearm while the wrist stays relaxed, allowing the hand and stick to flow loosely. The taps will be played as Moeller upstrokes, where the stick happens to tap the drum or cymbal as the forearm lifts and the hand drops. In order to maximize the flow, do not stop the stick after the accent, but instead let the accent stroke flop somewhat so that its energy flows into the following tap. You should feel as if you're playing quarter notes with your forearm while your hand flops and a little rebound stroke drops in on the upbeats.

Now let's look at the fill-in hand (the one that often plays the snare drum on the drumset). This hand will play the fourteen rhythms provided, using the free-stroke technique. The free stroke is the easiest and best-sounding way to play consecutive notes at a uniform volume level (notes with no accent/tap variation). Free strokes are relaxed "dribbles" of the stick played with the wrist and fingers. The key is to play a relaxed stroke with good velocity and then let the stick rebound back up to where it started. If you find yourself needing to pick up the stick in order to return to the up position, that means either that tension in your hand is preventing the stick from rebounding freely or the last stroke in the series isn't being played into the drum with enough velocity such that it can rebound back up on its own.

So, what are these fourteen patterns? They're all of the combinations of 8th and 16th notes possible within a quarter note. They're common patterns, so they'll likely sound familiar. But the trick is to coordinate these patterns with the opposite hand's flowing ostinato. If the lead hand's Moeller whip-and-flop motion is at all affected by the fill-in hand's part, then the comfortable flow, timing, and groove will be lost. If the fill-in hand's rhythms are inaccurate, if they flam with the lead hand, or if they're played tightly, then, once again, musical feel will be sacrificed. You want to be able to execute all of these patterns while watching each hand play its part comfortably and perfectly along with the opposite hand.

Be sure to practice the following two-hand coordination patterns with a metronome or play them along with your favorite tunes, and do not go any faster than you can play comfortably. Play each pattern for at least five minutes, making sure that there are no flams between the hands before speeding up to the next tempo. For part of the practice session, I recommend splitting up the hands on different playing surfaces so that you can analyze and perfect each hand's motion. When it comes time to play the patterns on the drumkit, try placing the lead hand on the ride cymbal, with the accents played on the bell and the taps on the bow. This application will make it easy to determine whether or not the coordination is working. Finally, make sure you also switch the hands so that the opposite hand is leading. Whether you think it's practical or not, learning to lead with either hand will make you a better player when you go back to leading with your usual hand.

For an additional challenge, try moving the accent in the lead hand to the upbeats.

16TH-NOTE RIDE

In Bonus Section 1, we looked at some two-hand coordination exercises where the lead hand played accented 8th notes with a Moeller whip-and-flop technique against fourteen basic duple-meter patterns in the opposite hand. Now we'll be using two common 16th-note ostinatos in the lead hand.

The ostinatos are to be played as loose rebounding free strokes, and they will require more finger control as the tempo increases. The opposite hand plays the fourteen basic duple-meter patterns using free strokes. This may seem simple at first, but to play the rhythms perfectly together—with both hands flowing and relaxed, and with no flams—is easier said than done. The key is to coordinate the hands so that each is seemingly unaware of what the other is doing, yet they're in perfect unison.

First let's look at the lead hand, which is the one you most often use for playing the hi-hat or ride cymbal. The "1-e-&" and "1, &-a" rhythms will be played as free strokes using the alley-oop-oop technique, which involves a wrist-finger-finger combination of free strokes. The first stroke is played mainly from the wrist, and the second and third strokes are played mainly from the fingers. This keeps the wrist from getting stressed out. Since so much finger control is necessary, you may find it preferable to play these patterns using the French grip—with the palm sideways and the thumb on top of the stick—since that hand position gives the fingers a wider range of motion and better access to the stick. French grip also allows for a more articulate stick-click sound.

The opposite hand plays the fourteen rhythms using free strokes. This technique is the easiest and best-sounding way to play consecutive notes at a uniform volume level (notes with no accent/tap variation). Free strokes are relaxed dribbles of the stick played with the wrist and fingers. The key is to play a smooth stroke with good velocity into the drum and then let the stick rebound freely back up to where it started. If you find yourself needing to pick up the stick after it strikes the drumhead, then there's either tension in the hand or the last stroke in the series wasn't played with enough velocity into the drum to allow the stick to rebound back up on its own.

The fourteen rhythms are all of the combinations of 8th and 16th notes possible within a quarter note. They're all common patterns, and they will probably sound familiar. But the trick is to coordinate these patterns with the opposite hand's flowing ostinato. You want to be able to play through these patterns while watching each hand play its part in perfect unison with the other.

Be sure to practice the following exercises with a metronome (or play them along with your favorite tunes), and don't go any faster than you can play comfortably using relaxed technique. Play each pattern for at least five minutes, making sure that there are no flams between the hands, before speeding up to the next tempo. For part of your practice session, I recommend splitting the hands on different playing surfaces so that you can analyze and perfect each hand's motion. Finally, make sure that you also switch the hands so that the opposite hand is leading, and feel free to add accents on the 8th notes.

Now switch the leading hand's ostinato to "1-&-a."

TRIPLET-BASED RIDE

Now let's shift into triplet mode. We'll combine the two most commonly used triplet-based ostinatos—the jazz ride and the shuffle—with the eight possible triplet-based rhythms.

Your hands will sometimes be playing with different techniques, yet they will have to remain completely relaxed. The key is to coordinate the hands so that each is seemingly unaware of what the other is doing, yet they're playing together perfectly without hitting any unwanted flams. Mastering these exercises will greatly increase your vocabulary and will undoubtedly manifest itself in different contexts in your playing.

First let's look at the jazz ride ostinato, which you most often use on the ride cymbal. Every note in this pattern should be played as a loose rebounding free stroke to maximize flow and to achieve the most resonant stick sound. I recommend playing the ride cymbal using French grip, since the vertical hand position (with the thumb on top) gives the fingers a wider range of motion and better access to the stick. French grip also lets the stick breathe more, which results in a more articulate stick-click sound. The stick should be in constant motion within a loose hand. Avoid picking the stick up after each stroke. It may take some time to develop the finger control necessary to dribble the stick so that it pops up by itself.

Now let's look at the fill-in hand, which most often plays the snare drum. This hand will also use the free stroke technique as it plays the eight triplet-based rhythms. The free stroke is the easiest and best-sounding way to play consecutive notes at a uniform volume level (notes with no accent/tap variation). Free strokes are relaxed dribbles of the stick played with the wrist and fingers. The key is to play a relaxed stroke with good velocity into the drum and

then let the stick freely rebound back up to where it started. If you find yourself needing to pick up the stick, that means there's either tension in the hand or the last stroke in the series wasn't played with enough velocity into the drum.

The eight triplet-based rhythms consist of all of the possible combinations within a quarter note and the two quarter-note-triplet patterns (starting on the downbeat and the upbeat). The objective is to coordinate these patterns with the opposite hand's ostinato without disrupting the flow. If the lead hand's motion is affected when you add the other hand, then the flow, timing, and groove will be lost. If the fill-in rhythms are played tightly or inaccurately (creating unwanted flams), feel will be sacrificed. You want to be able to play each of these patterns while observing the hands, making sure they are comfortable and perfectly in sync.

Practice the following coordination patterns with a metronome (or play them along with your favorite tunes), and don't go any faster than you can play comfortably using relaxed finger control. Play each pattern for at least five minutes, making sure that there are no flams between the hands before moving to the next tempo. (If you can't have a conversation with someone while playing these patterns, you're not ready to move on.)

For part of your practice session, I recommend splitting the hands on different playing surfaces so you can analyze and perfect each hand's motion individually. Finally, be sure to switch the hands so that the opposite hand is leading. Whether you think it's practical or not, learning to lead with the opposite hand will make you a better player when you go back to playing with your normal hand leading.

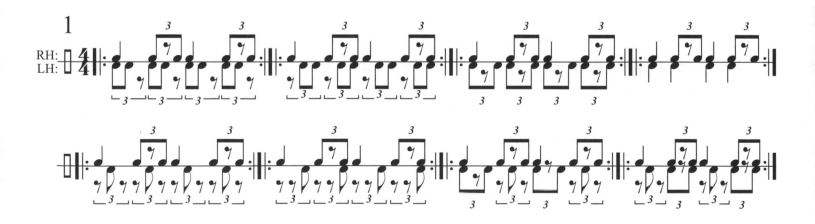

Now let's switch the lead hand's ostinato to the shuffle pattern.

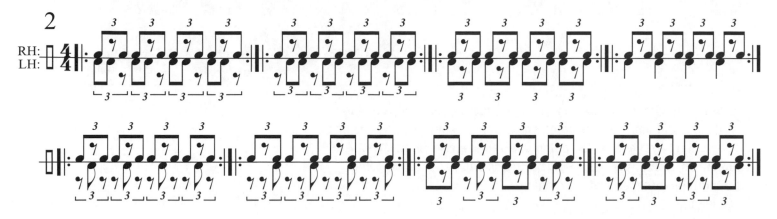

You can play the shuffle pattern without accents, but it's also common to play the shuffle pattern with an accent on the downbeat and a tap on the third partial of the triplet. To get a strong accent immediately following the low tap, you'll want to play the accents with the Moeller whip stroke. Think of the tap as a Moeller upstroke, where the stick just happens to hit the drum or cymbal as the arm is lifted and the hand and stick drop limp. Then throw the forearm down, causing the stick to whip back to the drum or cymbal with high velocity. The arm essentially drags the relaxed hand and stick up and down. The key is to not engage the wrist muscles during this motion, because that will cause excess tension and will make the system seize up.

When the lead hand is on the hi-hats, I recommend playing the tap with the bead of the stick on top of the cymbal and the accent on the edge with the shoulder of the stick. When you're playing the ride cymbal, the taps could be played with the bead of the stick on the bow, while the accents could be played with the shoulder of the stick on the bell.

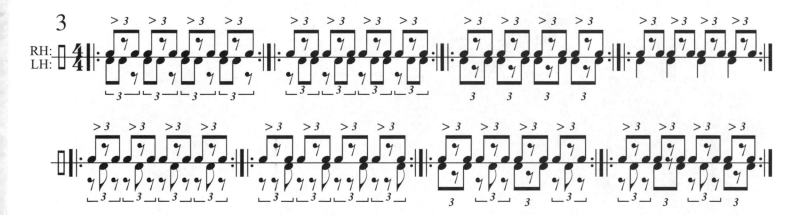

STICK TECHNIQUE
Wrap-Up

Congratulations on making it through *Stick Technique*! (You didn't cheat, did you?) At this point, you're ready to go back to page one and do it all over again. The rudiments and exercises in this book are fundamental and timeless, and your hands will benefit from going through the material again and again.

Have fun!

Leslie Voorheis